Dear Mum & Dad

Gemini

A small lockdown project only — that I had no idea it could be so much fun doing this!

Lucky you doing it for real!!

Mark G

Dear Mum & Dad

Letters Home from Active Service
1941-1945

Dennis Gwynne MC. TD.
Edited by Mark Gwynne

MENSCH
Mensch Publishing

Mensch Publishing
51 Northchurch Road, London N1 4EE, United Kingdom

First published in Great Britain 2020

ISBN: paperback – 978-1-912914-19-7
e-book – 978-1-912914-20-3

Typeset by Van-garde Imagery, Inc., Florida, United States

For those to who gave their
todays for our tomorrows.

And for those who did come home again to
live quiet lives, but are no longer here to tell
us their extraordinary stories.

And to my father, Michael Gwynne, who
still goes to the office that Robert built
and where Reg, Norman, Leslie and
Dennis all worked.

Contents

Introduction xi

1941 1

1942 7

1943 65

1944 101

1945 147

Acknowledgements 195

'Mum and Dad' - Robert and Winifred Gwynne at Eversleigh
House, Wellington, Shropshire

DENNIS HERBERT GWYNNE (DHG) was born on 2 August 1919 in Wellington, Shropshire, the eighth and youngest child of Robert and Winifred Gwynne.

Of his siblings, Reginald was born in 1901, Mary in 1905, Leslie in 1907, Norman in 1908, Elizabeth (or Betty) in 1913, Dorothy (or Dorrie) in 1914 and Barbara in 1916.

He was educated at Shrewsbury School, and articled at the family law firm, R. Gwynne & Sons in which had been founded by Robert Gwynne in 1908.

Dennis was commissioned in 4th Battalion, King's Shropshire Light Infantry (KSLI) in August, 1939. Together with his older brothers, Leslie and Norman, he was sent to India on attachment to the Indian Army in 1942. His sister, Barbara, served in the Women's Auxiliary Air Force (WAAF).

Reg Gwynne, who was thirty-eight years old at the start of the war, stayed at home and ran the family firm with his father, Robert. Robert was approaching his sixty-seventh birthday when Leslie, Norman and Dennis were posted to India in 1942.

Introduction

I NEVER INTENDED TO write this book. Actually, I never imagined I would ever write any sort of book at all. *Dear Mum & Dad* really started out as a history project to give my teenage sons something to discuss with their grandfather on a regular basis during the COVID lockdown. It was also meant to assuage my guilt for having done nothing with Dennis's letters except leave them in a desk draw for several years.

As the weeks went by, I began to spend as many hours in the day as I possibly could with Dennis, pausing only for cups of coffee and to stretch aching limbs. I became immersed in his letters and photographs, frantically trying to make up for lost time and desperate to fill in the gaps between what was actually happening to him and what he was telling his family in his letters home. Along the way I was able to find answers to many questions. But some, frustratingly, I was forced to leave unanswered as the trails ran cold and the facts stayed tantalisingly beyond living memory or unarchived.

By the time I finished, I realised why I had never wanted to write a book before. I have never liked the sound of my own voice enough to expect that anyone would be interested enough to listen. But Dennis solved that problem for me as they are his words, not mine and *Dear Mum & Dad* is the result of our collaboration. My only regret is that I didn't think of doing it before.

My own memories of Dennis are a little hazy. I was only six years old when he died and my brother Simon, his godson, was only three. I do vividly recall, however, his glass eye which my father kept after Dennis died. I was always told that this was a special "bloodshot one" that he wore to match with his good one when he had been out for a few drinks.

I was, from a young age, always led to believe that Dennis had been the life and soul of all the best parties. He has certainly been truly excellent company for me during these last few months and I like to think we have become quite close. I can now read his handwriting with almost total accuracy and even mimic his style of letter writing.

He is witty and modest and his observations are well made and often very detailed. He has shared generously his experiences of wartime in India and Burma, with literally hundreds of letters and telegrams, maps and photos. There are so many hidden gems and insights into the last years of Colonial India, the Bengal famine, the Gurkhas and life on active service in Slim's Forgotten Army.

Most fascinatingly for me, he has brought to life people I have heard so much about, but either barely remember or never met. He has taken the time to answer a lot of my questions about our family, and raised a few more.

Dennis was a very brave man and an accomplished soldier. His obituary in the *Bugle & Kukri* journal of May 1973 noted:

> *Of the Regiment's World War II Battle Honours … Dennis Gwynne, whilst commanding 'B' Company, played a conspicuous part in winning two - Imphal and Tuitum - a worthy epitaph surely for any soldier, professional or amateur, and one with which Dennis would have been well content.*

But my sense above all else is of an incredibly dutiful son, a loyal brother, a generous friend and a proud Salopian – his excitement on getting back copies of the *Wellington Journal* is palpable!

His concern for his parents' health and wellbeing is always his primary focus and particularly striking is the contrast in between the continual reassurance he is giving them in his letters throughout 1943/44 and the reality of the intense jungle fighting in the Burma Campaign, particularly from February to May 1944 at Imphal.

For all his much-lauded success as a soldier, his sole motivation was to do his job, to get home, to get on with being "plain Mister" once more and to finally finish his articles at the family law firm, R. Gwynne & Sons.

1941

ONE YEAR ON FROM Dunkirk and the Battle of Britain, the threat of imminent invasion from mainland Europe had materially diminished. In June 1941, Germans forces launched Operation Barbarossa on the Eastern Front, the code name for the invasion of the Soviet Union. The eventual failure of this campaign would be a crucial turning point in the war.

In mid-1941, DHG was deployed on home defence duties with 5 KSLI, on attachment from his own Battalion, 4 KSLI.

4 KSLI 1939 – Dennis Gwynne is 4th from left in the front row

2 August 1941

5 KSLI, Fontwell, nr Arundel, Sussex.

Dear Mum and Dad,

Thank you very much for your letters and presents. Stanley [Corbett] arrived back safely last night and gave them to me. Did you get the parcel of laundry as well? We are still very busy down here. There is much to be done and we have quite a large mileage of coast to cover and guard day and night. There is no such day as Sunday for us now. We work seven days a week and we are allowed a half day when it can be managed, which isn't very often. I managed to get one today as it is my birthday. It doesn't seem a year since you came to London to see me, does it? I saw Norman last night for a short while. He rang me up and asked if I would go over to his place for a bit as he was feeling fed up and wants to get out for a change. He is just this side of Bognor about four miles from me.

Do you remember David Allen-Williams who was at Aldenham with me?[1] I went to stay with him in Littlehampton one summer holiday. I thought I would go there this afternoon to see his parents and find out what he's doing. I expect he is in one of the services

---

1   Aldenham Park prep school, near Bridgnorth, Shropshire.

somewhere. Please don't forget to send my other Sam Browne when you post the laundry back, Mum.[2]

On 7 December, 1941, the Imperial Japanese Navy launched a surprise air strike on Pearl Harbour.

Japan intended the attack as a preventive action to keep the United States Pacific Fleet from interfering with its planned military actions in Southeast Asia. Over the course of seven hours, there were coordinated Japanese attacks on Singapore, Hong Kong, Thailand, Malaysia and the Philippines.

The attack at Pearl Harbour led to the US formally declaring war on Japan the next day.

Under the terms of the Tripartite Agreement signed by the Axis powers on 27 September 1940, Germany and Italy declared war on the US on 11 December 1941.

---

2 The Sam Browne was the standard issue British Army Officer's leather waist belt with diagonal right shoulder strap, named after 19th Century British Indian Army General, Sir Sam Browne, who designed the belt to enable time to draw his sword one handed having lost his left arm in the Sepoy Rebellion of 1857.

24 December 1941

Telegram

Every good wish to you all for a happy Xmas.
Parcels received. Delighted with contents. Please
pass message to all friends around the Wrekin,

love[3]

---

3 'To all friends around the Wrekin' is an old Shropshire toast.

1942

6 January 1942
Abbey Gate House, Sherborne Dorset.

Dear Mum and Dad,

The above address is only my billet so don't think I have moved again. Actually, we are moving the Officers' Mess up to Sherbourne Castle shortly and will be all together again up there. Thank you for your letters and parcels. We had an officers' dance here on New Year's Eve and let the New Year in in the usual manner. Graham and Nora [Murphy] were there and have since gone on leave. I suppose you knew that Graham is now a Lieutenant, bad luck for him, isn't it? I have at last managed to find out what happened to Norman. I kept asking you why he was on leave again and all you would say was that he was going away!! I rang up the 2nd Herefords and they told me he was going to India.[1]

---

1 Herefordshire Light Infantry – Norman's regiment and sister regiment to KSLI.

I only wish I could get abroad myself instead of messing about like we are all the time. It's a wonder we haven't got Home Guard written on our shoulders!

Now that Christmas and New Year is all over, we are settled down to the usual stuff again. It has been extremely cold here this last week and my sheepskin has come in very handy and keeps me nice and warm. The cake you sent was well accepted by the mess and went down very well.

British forces in Singapore surrendered on 15 February 1942.

Prime Minister Winston Churchill described the fall of Singapore as "the worst disaster and largest capitulation in British history." Singapore had long been a strategic prize as part of the key shipping route between Asia and Europe.

The Japanese claimed to have taken more than 60,000 Imperial troops prisoner in Singapore - 16,000 British, 14,000 Australian and 32,000 Indian soldiers.

Meanwhile, in the British colony of Burma, after nearly three months of fighting the Burma Army evacuated Rangoon on 7 March. As they left, they implemented a scorched earth plan, destroying the port and the oil terminal so that they could not be used by the Japanese.

From early 1942, Britain and the Commonwealth began sending as many men, arms and munitions to India as could be spared in the face of the speed and success of the Japanese campaigns in SE Asia.

DHG was posted as 'British Service Attached' or 'BSA' to the Indian Army, as distinct to the British Army in India.

It may be that DHG was selected because of a small 'disciplinary issue' involving the use of army rationed petrol for his car. This would be in line with anecdotes from other BSA officers as to why they were selected by their underlying units (including his brother, Norman, whose men accidentally burned down a thatched barn belonging to a local farmer on the south coast of England).

The Indian Army had a mix of Indian and British officers and Indian other ranks. There was a variety of different types of commission, depending on the nationality but also the status of the officer concerned.[2]

8 March 1942
The Grand Hotel, Charing Cross, Glasgow

Dear Mum and Dad,

The above will be my address until I sail. We are very comfortable here and I have met lots of fellows I know already. There is not a great deal for us to do, except in the mornings when we have a lecture. I had a

---

2 At the time of the fall of Singapore, the Indian Army numbered around 200,000 men but was to become the largest volunteer army ever assembled. By August 1945, it numbered in excess of 2.5 million men and women at arms. The Indian Army served in the Far East, North Africa and European theatres of war between 1939-45. More than 87,000 Indian Empire service personnel lost their lives overall in WWII.

very good journey up to Glasgow with another fellow I met at Crewe from the 4th Battalion KSLI. Vera got me there in good time, the roads being quite good. All my luggage is now safely in store here until I want it.

P.S. When you address my letters, don't put my number or regiment.

14 March 1942

I have given Lena [Norman Gwynne's wife] the policy for the car together with the registration book and have no other papers regarding it at all. Glad to hear Les has landed OK. I expect by now he will know that I am on the way, too. Let me know Norman's address as soon as you know it. The weather is not so bad and we spend a lot of our time wandering around the town.

15 March 1942

Heard from Cox & King and they have opened my account with the £25 I sent them. I am ready for the fray. No news yet and having so much spare time on our hands is getting boring. I don't think I have ever written home so many times in a week before!! If I stop here any longer, I will be speaking with a Scotch accent. It gets very monotonous when you hear it all day long wherever you go. Glasgow itself has a peculiarly broad accent, which is a bit difficult at first.

19 March 1942

I have received my watch and it appears to be working quite well. I have got my new address and that will be the one until you hear from me again. I don't quite know when that will be. I'm sorry to hear you had not been well, Dad, and hope by now you are better.

I wish I could be at home to lend a hand and look after you both. Thinking of you and looking forward to the time when we shall all be together again. Please don't worry about me, you know I shall be alright.

By 1942, a voyage to India via the Mediterranean and the Suez Canal was not possible. Rommel's Afrika Korps launched an offensive in North Africa in February 1942 and German Luftwaffe and U Boat activity intensified in the Eastern Mediterranean, focused on Malta.

Ships en route to India, therefore, were forced to travel via Cape Town, often zig zagging into the Atlantic, and refuelling in various ports on the west African coast. It took DHG's ship six weeks to get to Cape Town, rather than the usual two weeks in peacetime owing to U Boat activity.

Passenger ships travelling to and from Cape Town had been sunk as far west as Ascension Island and St Helena. On leaving Cape Town, shipping was less vulnerable as the

British Fleet was head quartered in East Africa from early 1942.

30 March 1942
Ship Mail from D.H. Gwynne, KSLI

Dear Mum and Dad,

It seems ages since I left home and I am missing your usual letters. I think about you all at home a lot and wonder how you are and what you are doing. I am very well and fit and also getting quite brown. The sun is extremely hot and we have been sunbathing in small doses so as to get used to it slowly. I share a cabin with five others. Things are, of course, a bit cramped but we manage quite well except in the mornings when there is a bit of a scramble for the wash basin and bath.

I have found some very good fellows on the boat and I'm well off in that respect. We have had no really rough weather yet and I have felt no ill effects and have not missed a single meal. In fact, I think I'm eating more than ever. The sea air is very invigorating and makes us very hungry.

After about four days I found my sea legs and now don't notice the movement at all. It felt a bit strange at first, being in bed with the cabin gently swaying, but then we got used to it. If you think my writing is worse than usual put it down to the movement of the boat!! Not much for us to do during the day except read and wander around and I have read ten books already. Every morning and afternoon we have the language, which I am picking up fairly quickly.[3] It's rather like being back at school, doing the verbs etc. and standing up to translate a passage from the book.

Washing is a bit of a problem on the boat – we have to do it in the bath! Sea water is useless and we have to carry water from the basin in a jug to fill up the bath. I did a pair of pyjamas and two shirts yesterday and I'm going to iron them tonight when I get near the iron. There's usually a long queue waiting for it. I realise now what you must feel like after a washing day, although mine only took me about an hour to do. I bought myself a packet of 'Rinso', which I believe is the right stuff to use. Anyway, the things look quite clean again. There is an excellent canteen on the boat where we can buy more or less anything we want. There is also quite a large library.

---

3 All BSA officers had to learn Urdu - the main language spoken in the Indian Army.

Good Sunday, 5 April 1942

Just had breakfast with hot X buns and wondered if you did same.

It continues to get hotter every day and getting to sleep at night is rather difficult. We all long to be able to jump over the side and have a swim around. The water is a perfect blue and we spend a lot of time looking over the side watching porpoise, turtle and flying fish etc. I have not seen a shark yet. There are games of deck tennis and shuffle board. By the way, one of my cabin companions was at Sandhurst with Norman and knows him quite well.

Date Unknown, March to May 1942

You will be pleased to hear that I am very fit and enjoying the voyage. I seem to be getting browner every day. We shall be calling in at the next port of call in a few days and will be getting a chance to post some letters again. Did you receive the last one OK?

There's not much to say as nearly every subject is banned and we have to be very careful. I'm going to try and get a cable off home and also to Les when we put in at the next port, so watch out for one.

How is everyone at home? I have written about ten letters to all the various members of the family and also one or two outside. I hope you are well, Dad, and not overdoing things. It must be terribly hard pegging for you and Reg at the office and I hope it won't be long before we are all back to help you with things.

We have the BBC News relayed every day so we are not completely out of touch with the old home country. I often wonder when I'm listening whether you are as well. How is Babs getting on?

We still keep on with our language classes and I'm picking it up quite well now. By the time I arrive I should be able to speak it fairly well, well enough to get along anyway. I shall be glad when we get there and will be able to get down to some work again. The inactivity on board gets a bit boring sometimes and the daily routine is slightly monotonous.

A list of phrases which we can use in our cables has been posted up but they do not seem to be much use. It's OK for the married men cabling to their wives, but not much use for chaps like me just cabling home. Anyway, as long as you get some sort of message you will know that I am fit and well. I have met several more fellows since I last wrote to you including two from Shrewsbury and one from Oswestry. Altogether, we have a very good crowd on board and that makes things much better and the time passes more quickly. In the evenings, we mostly sit about in the lounge playing cards or reading. Thank goodness the ship has a good library. I think I have read half the books in it already!

27 April 1942

Letter from Grand Hotel, Cape Town, from Margaret C. Black

Dear Mr & Mrs Gwynne,

I don't suppose you will know who I am, but your son, Dennis, passed through here and has spent the last four days here. As they are not allowed to write I said I would send you a line to let you know he is fit and well, I must say he looks well. He and three other friends spent a good deal of time here and we tried to make it as happy as we could. They even came to a hockey match – I may add I train teachers for Physical Education – so as they spent their leave here, they thought they might like to watch 'the girls' play hockey. I think both the students and the 'Boys' enjoyed themselves. You have a delightful son and he is so full of life – he says he is "fighting fit" and he looks it.

I think they were all very bored with the voyage, as they took six weeks to get to here – it seems awful as we, in peace time, get here in thirteen days. Mrs Richer, who owns this hotel, is very good to all the boys. We are both from home – Mrs Richer is from Richmond and I am from Scotland – so you could imagine when we have a convoy here it is like being at home again, and getting news direct is marvellous.

I have sent a cable from Dennis to your other son in India. Your son hasn't left yet, but they are not ashore today, but are lying out in the Bay – I can imagine how peeved they are at being so near and yet so far. Dennis sends his love and heaps of messages to both of you.

9 May 1942
Telegram - Sent sans origine:

All well and safe. Love. Keep smiling

The Grand Hotel, Cape Town

23 May 1942

Aerograph

I was delighted when I found I was being sent to Mhow, and I found Leslie the same afternoon that we arrived.[4] I shall be here for about two months on a language course and will then be posted to regiment. I was very glad to hear you are all well. I am longing to get a letter from you myself. I have cabled Norman. The weather here is very hot now and I have not yet got properly used to it. We have fairly comfortable quarters under canvas and a Mess under canvas too. I am glad the journey is over even though I enjoyed it all. Can you ring up Mrs Corbett so she can tell Stanley? I will write to him.

---

4   Mhow is approx 350 miles from Mumbai – or 15-20hrs by rail. The city was renamed 'Dr. Ambedkar Nagar' in 2003 and is in the Indore district in the Indian state of Madhya Pradesh. Some say Mhow stood for "Military Headquarters of War". However, this is a "backronym".

British Army Infantry Barracks at Mhow taken pre WW1, was the location of the tented camp Dennis was sent to on arrival in India in 1942.

It is over 5,500 nautical miles from Cape Town to Mumbai, so we can assume that DHG arrived some time before 20 May 1942 depending on the speed of the convoy and the number of ports of call. Margaret Black refers in her letter to convoy(s) arriving in Cape Town.

Interestingly, there was a Times of India headline written on 3 June 1942 entitled "Biggest British Troop Convoy Ever Reaches India", which was also filmed on arrival by Pathé News. The convoy arrived without incident and this must have been sometime before 3 June, when the press report appeared, in order to let the troops unload and disperse. So, it could even have tallied with DHG's arrival around 20 May.

Article in Times of India – 3 June 1942

Undated June 1942
Telegram – O wing OTS, Mhow

Same camp as Les, Love

Self outside my bungalow tent at O.T.S. Mhow, May 1942. The roofing over the tents is for extra protection from the sun. Les was in one like this about 200 yards from mine.

15 June 1942

Aerograph from Mhow

I was very glad to get your cable and to know you are well. We have settled down and are getting on with the work. I have had a letter from Norman and am seeing quite a lot of Les. He will be leaving here soon. I am very fit and well and looking forward to your first letter. It seems years since I heard from you. The weather is cooling down now and the monsoon is just starting.

'Me and our Den' – Dennis and Leslie Gwynne, Mhow
May/June 1942

24 June 1942
Telegram - Lloyds Bank, Bombay.

Fit and well, Love

---

26 June 1942
Lloyds Bank Bombay.

Dear Mum and Dad,

So far, I have not had any mail from home and am anxiously waiting for a letter. I am very lucky being in the same camp as Les because I can read your letters to him and get all the home news. Unfortunately, I am being posted to my regiment – I don't know which one it is to be yet – on Monday next (30th June) so will be saying goodbye to him temporarily. I have seen a good deal of him while I have been in Mhow, and it has been very nice to be together so far from home.

I have had two letters from Norman in Peshawar. He seems to be doing very well and should get a Majority fairly soon. I do not know when I shall get my Captaincy back, as things are not quite as we were told before we left. I shall probably have to wait for a while as I have had no experience in the Indian army yet. Still,

I'm not worrying about it as out here I get almost the same pay as a Lieutenant as I did at home as a Captain.

We are in the middle of the monsoon and everything is very wet and sticky. The ground gets very boggy. Mhow itself is really a low hill station, so we get both the plains and the hills. The jungle is fairly thick here, although not as much as in some parts. I have been out on one shooting trip so far lasting three days and we had quite a lot of sport. We were guests of a local Rajah and he treated us very well and it was a good way to learn about the country and the natives, or the 'Wogs" as we call them.

At the moment, we are all living in tents which have a sort of wicker roof over them to keep off the heat. They are not bad really – the floors are made of cow dung and straw and of course the ants and bugs get everywhere. At night we have to sleep in mosquito nets which are fixed over the beds on a wooden frame. The top of the net is about four feet above the bed. The business of getting into bed is a bit complicated. First, you lift up one side and chase away any flies and mosquitos which may be inside. Then you tuck the bottoms under the mattress very carefully so that no more can get in. If a mosquito is inside you will never get to sleep until it is dead or outside and, by that time, you've probably been bitten.

After four days of being here I got some sort of fever and had seven days in hospital, but I wasn't really very ill. I think it was probably the heat more than anything else.

The Urdu is coming along quite well and I can now usually make myself understood. A lot of the natives speak English, but we have to know it fairly well to train the men. R100 reward when we do, which is worth about £8.

The presents I have sent you I bought in the native bazaar (shopping centre) and are really genuine handmade silk. They were very cheap, but at home they would be worth about £15 each. I actually paid £5 for each of them (about 93 Rupees). I thought perhaps Babs would like one. You may have to pay a bit of duty on them because I have insured the parcel, but it won't be too much.

The bazaar is in a small town like Mhow, which is far more interesting than in the larger ones which are usually fairly westernised. Everything you buy you haggle over the price for about a quarter of an hour, otherwise you'll get badly done. Whatever the man wants – say 20 Rupees – you immediately say 10 and then you start and go on until you are satisfied. A good trick is to say no and walk out and he'll come running after you and cut the price down to your figure. Everywhere you go there are children and beggars shouting "Backsheesh

Sahib" (tips) and if you do give one of them anything you will never get rid of the others.

All transport is done by Tonga, which is like a pony and trap with a little awning over the top, heavy stuff is taken in bullock carts. We ourselves use bicycles to get around, otherwise it would cost us a fortune in Tonga charges.

I have to give this letter to the shopkeeper to put in with your parcel and it is quite a long way to the bazaar. The bazaar usually comprises all the native quarter and the military quarter is called the cantonment. Hope the parcel reaches you safely – I think it should take about ten weeks – I wonder where I will be by then. Wherever I am, I shall be thinking of you and home and hoping to be on my way back to you soon – you and Reg must be very overworked and I hope you are not overdoing it.

Indore State Army Race – Mhow 1942 the state army is the Rajah's own private army now fighting for us. These are two of the men, taken at a race meeting in Mhow.

When leaving Mhow, all officers are given these garlands of wild flowers by their bearers, as a token of good luck.

Bagli May 1942 – while on Shikar *(note: a hunt)* we came to this village which was very proud of its elephant. It used to be a Rajahs's elephant, note the gold bands around the end of its tusks, but was now too old.

28 June 1942

Aerograph

Just got letters 1,2 and 3 from Dad and number 1 from Mum. I was very happy to be able to hear from you after so long and know that you are both well. Today we have been posted to our new Regts and I am going to the Gurkha Rifles. I don't know yet which Bn. I shall be writing to Stanley Corbett and Ted James myself. I shall be sorry to be moved away from Leslie, but hope to see him and Norman again when I get leave. I am very fit and well and my pay has come through so I'm ok for money. Keep smiling.

10th Gurkha Rifles (10 GR) was formed in 1890. In WWII it had four Battalions. Of these, the 1st, 3rd and 4th were heavily involved with the Burma Campaign of 1942-1945 against the Japanese.

The 1st Battalion arrived in Burma just before the fall of Rangoon in March 1942 and conducted a fighting retreat over hundreds of miles, reaching India in May 1942 – the month before DHG was posted to the Regiment.

The Regiment's four Battalions spent more time in action and won more gallantry awards than any other regiment in the Indian Army in WWII, with more than 1,000 dead and 2,000 wounded.

In total, 250,280 Gurkhas served in forty Battalions in the British Army, earning over 2,734 bravery awards and suffering around 32,000 casualties in all theatres.

6 July 1942

Aerograph – Alhilal, Kangra Valley, Punjab:[5]

I have been posted to 10 GR and am at their depot. When I have learned their language, which is Gurkhali, not Urdu as we were learning at Mhow, I will be posted to one of their four battalions.

---

5   The Kangra Valley is in the Western Himalayas in the Indian state of Himachal Pradesh in the Punjab. It is about 850 miles north of Mhow and 125 miles from western Tibet. The valley floor has an average elevation of 2000ft.

We are stationed in the foothills of the Himalayas, very wild and about ninety miles from any town, although there are several native villages nearby, in a tented camp which is under construction. The country is very pretty and thickly wooded. The Regt Centre is more or less like our old Salop depot – mainly recruit training – and then they are passed on to line battalions.[6] Only Gurkhas of course, who come from Nepal and are extremely fine mountain fighters. I have been given the job as Transport Officer, but am trying to get away to a battalion as soon as I can manage the language. All Gurkha Regiments speak Gurkali and don't understand Indian, so we can only use Urdu with Indians.

Actually, the Indian officers (Viceroy commissioned, equivalent to our sergeant-majors) can usually speak Urdu and a little English, so it's not really as difficult as it seems.[7]

The monsoon is now up here and it is very wet. The mountain streams in full flow make wonderful sights. The hills abound with lots of animals and the shooting is very good although I don't expect to have time for that now, I'd rather get on with the job. But too wet

---

6   the Copthorne Barracks in Shrewsbury, which was the KSLI depot from its formation in 1881

7   A Viceroy's Commission as distinct from a King's Commission for British officers, who would rank senior to any Gurkha officer irrespective of the Gurkha officer's rank).

now in any case.

I stopped at Delhi for forty-eight hours leave on the way up from Mhow. I went into a hotel and walked straight into Les again – a grand impulse! He is doing very well in his new job and says he will have another pip shortly.

30 July 1942

Telegram – Alhilal Camp, Kangra Valley.

AG Received. Everything fine. Letters Sent, Love.

---

30 July 1942

10 GR, Alhilal Camp, Kangra Valley

Dear Mum and Dad,

I have just received mail after one month without after regular mail at Mhow, so it may be that the sharks had them instead.

Yesterday, Lloyds Bombay wrote to say £18-17s-6d received from Cox & Kings in London. I don't know what the money is for, but am hanging on to it and keeping quiet. It may be that the British army is still paying me and this is my pay for June, in which case I expect I still have to pay it back. They have done that in many cases and the unfortunate officers suddenly find themselves having to pay back about six months' pay. Being paid twice not so funny when you have to pay it back after it has been spent.

I've settled in pretty well now and I'll be glad to be back at work after such a long period of inactivity. I am very lucky to have been posted to the Ghurkha Rifles as they are easily the finest regiment in the Indian army and mark well up with Regiments like the Guards at home. Actually, they are not Indian at all but come from Nepal, which is an independent state north of the Himalaya Mountains and their army is employed by the British government here to fight for the Empire.

They have already made a wonderful name in Burma and Libya and, as I say, I feel very proud to be with them. The officers are British with some Gurkha officers in each company (who are about equivalent to our own Sergeant-Majors in the British army). The men themselves are extremely nice fellows, mostly completely unspoiled by western ideas – such things as dishonesty and deceit etc. never seem to enter their heads, chiefly because they don't know what they are and have never had any use for them. They are always marvellously faithful.

I've been very lucky with my personal orderly as I have found one who speaks Urdu as well as Gurkhali, so that I can talk to him fairly easily. He's very good and keeps all my things in proper order and does all my washing and ironing, gets my food in Mess and generally keeps me on the straight and narrow!!

This washing business is rather funny – the orderly goes to the river, or wherever the nearest water is, and washes the things with soap, then hangs them on a hook and keeps them hanging until they are clean. The marvel of it is that the clothes never suffer, even silk never seems to get torn or worn away by it. He does the ironing with an old flat iron on a piece of board.

The camp here is now almost finished, that is as a tented camp, and has turned out quite a large place, of course. As a training centre for four battalions we are dealing with something up to 5,000 recruits in the camp at one time. The recruits are all bought down from Nepal and seeing them with some clothes on for the first time is really funny. All they wear in the jungle is a sort of loin cloth. When they put on boots for the first time it looks as though they are carrying a ton of weight on each foot and it takes about a month to get used to them.

The district we are in is very beautiful, being among the foothills of the Himalaya Mountains and about 4,500 ft up. I think I told you before that the nearest town, if that's what it could be called, is about ninety miles away. But we have many little villages nearer where we get odds and ends in the bazaars. These are usually a collection of four or five dirty little shops in the middle of the village, but it is nearly always possible to buy soap and the necessities of life. Rather like the outside market at home but a bit more colourful!! [**Wellington Market – really??!! -Ed**] Altogether, we don't do badly and have a good Mess here with wireless etc … and have little to spend our money on which is a good thing.

In the hills with some Gurkhas. The background on the right is more hills and cloud. Later on when the clouds cleared, we could see right down into the camp – about 5,000 ft below.

There's a very good crowd in the Mess, most of the fellows being emergency commissions from OTCs out here and at the moment I find myself fourth senior officer in terms of length of service, though not in rank.[8] The CO and two Majors are regulars and, of the others, I have been commissioned longest, though there are four captains here who have been promoted very soon after getting a commission. At the moment I don't see any prospect of getting my captaincy back as there is no vacancy. It's a bit annoying to have to take orders from someone you know is really about two years junior to you in the service.

At the moment I am assistant MTO, [Motor Transport Officer] which I am doing my best to get out of because the job has no prospects at all and I'm trying to get to a rifle company. If I can, I shall be posted to an active battalion much quicker, which is what I really want. The officers and men are drawn from the Regimental Centre by whichever Battalion of the Regiment wants reinforcements. As we have three Battalions of Regiment now in service, all the rifle company officers will stand a good chance of being required sooner or later. One officer, who came out on the boat with me and was posted up here, has gone already, chiefly because he speaks Burmese.

When we have passed the Urdu exam, we concen-

8 OTC or UOTC stands for Officer's Training Corps is a University based training organisation which still exists today. Sandhurst Royal Military Academy closed for Regular Commissions in 1939. One of the main routes into the Officer corps of the British Indian Army was via an OTC certificate and interview to assess suitability at the India Office.

trate on Gurkhali, which is the Gurkhas' own language. It is very similar to Urdu actually, so should not be very hard to pick up. We get plenty of practice every day as English is no good when speaking to the men. When you are absolutely stuck you have to resort to sign language or, failing that, get hold of another officer to help you (this latter considered very poor!)

The monsoon is still here and will be until the end of August. It doesn't just rain, it simply falls down and such things as Mackintoshes are just useless. It's really best to let yourself get wet and then to change at night when the work is done instead of trying to keep dry with a Mackintosh, which is so hot and sticky. The men work in a pair of shorts and nothing else which is about the best dress, I think.

I'm always very thankful for a dry tent at the end of the day and old Balbadahur Sunwar my orderly, all ready with my bath and a clean set of clothes.[9]

By the way, our dress is very good. We wear shorts and a bush shirt which has big patch pockets and regimental bottoms (black), long stockings with boots and wide brimmed hat like the Australians – very comfortable and shady from the sun. In the evening we wear long trousers and shoes to keep the mosquitoes off your

---

9   Sunwar is a Gurkha tribe from East Nepal and most Gurkha's used tribal family names.

knees. They really are a pest up here at night and we have to be most careful with our nets to see they are properly tucked under the bedding all around.

Self and my orderly taken in Camp Oct 1942. His name is Balbahadur Sunwar aged 22 – has 2 sons aged 8 and 5!! I had just come out of the river, where I had been trying to keep cool. The hills in the background are the beginning of the Himalayas, though it was too cloudy to see much. The wall behind goes round the house of some local Rajah who lives there with his five wives, but his wives are all locked up and never allowed out because they might be seen by people of low caste, in which case they must commit suicide!!

We have a fairly long day starting at 6 am and finishing at about 5.30 pm and usually there is a break in the middle of the day for about two to three hours as it's almost impossible to work when it's hot, 100° in the shade, sometimes more.

I get letters from Les as well as Norman, fairly often, and I am looking forward to meeting them again. I met Les in Delhi on my way up here. He's certainly dropped on his feet with his new job. I will send some snaps soon. I had a bit of bad luck with my camera the other day. I was out with it in the rain and it got wet inside and the film got spoiled so I am sending it away to be cleaned. The damp gets into everything in this sort of weather. When the rain stops, my orderly puts everything out in the sun to dry – it is about the only way of stopping all the clothes from going mouldy.

Have you got Alan Benson's address? I know his home address in Admaston, but if I can find out where he is in Libya it will be much quicker than sending it all the way to England to be forwarded back again.

I wrote to Lena, Madge, Vera, Betty, Dorrie and Babs and I hope to get some replies soon. It is great when you get a letter as they are so few and far between so you have to imagine how welcome they are when they arrive.

14 August 1942
Aerograph

I received your cable the day after my birthday and have been hoping for a letter, but nothing has arrived for six weeks.

I have been in hospital for two weeks with dysentery, but am better now and back with the battalion and may get a few days sick leave and, if so, will probably go down to Simla to spend a few days with Les.[10] I had a letter from Norman the other day who was just moving to Bangalore. It is still raining very heavily and should finish in about three weeks. We are all looking forward to a chance to get our things out of the tents to dry. How is the office going, Dad? Hope you and Reg managing things?

15 August 1942
Aerograph

Just had your AG dated 5th July and one from Babs. Glad to hear you had a letter from Margaret Black.[11] We had a very good time there and they looked after us and showed us around etc. in the good old colonial style.

---

10 Simla or Shimla is the capital of the state Himachal Pradesh and was the Summer capital of British India and is about 130 miles from the Kangra Valley.
11 Cape Town letter of 27 April 1942.

I am feeling much better now and returning to camp tomorrow. I shall be glad to get back to work again. Have been out for a walk, but still feeling weak in the legs.

18 August 1942

Dear Mum and Dad,

I arrived back from Hospital yesterday and am now feeling more or less fit again. I have been given six days excused duty but I am not going down to Simla to see Les as I had hoped. One thing, it will take me most of that to get there and back and the other is that I have got to have my teeth seen to. So, I have got permission to go to Lahore which is only about one day's journey away. Two of my teeth need stopping –we get it done by the army dentist so I'm taking a chance while I can.

Lahore is not much of a place but it will be a nice change from here and it will be pleasant to see a bit of civilization again and to go to a flick etc. I will travel on a free rail warrant and I only have to pay for my hotel which is about six rupees or, in your language, 9s per day, which isn't bad.

When I got back to camp my tent was in a bit of a mess as my orderly had been away and nobody had been in and everything had got very damp and covered in mildew. Still we got them out into the sun and the rain stopped and nothing is any worse now, except a pair of slippers which had been left on the floor and the ants had eaten nearly the whole of one away. Unless something is right off the ground the ants will eat it – particularly leather. Even in one night they will go through the sole of the shoe.

We are looking forward to the end of the rains now they are due to finish in the first or second week in September. Then it will gradually get cooler until next March or April, when the hot weather starts again. Up in the hills here it will get cold enough for us to wear battle dress and service dress instead of shorts. We may even get snow. We can of course see plenty of snow now up in the mountains and in the cold weather it gradually creeps lower and lower. We are at about 4,500ft up so will probably get a bit.

My camera has been out of action. It got very damp and went a bit rusty inside and I have had to send it away. I hope to make a collection of snaps while I'm out here and they will be interesting to look back on in later years.

The other night I had a scare while in bed. I woke up about 3 am and felt something pulling at the outside of my mosquito net. I hadn't the foggiest what it was so I put my hand under the net and grabbed my torch off the little table by my bed. What I saw nearly made me die of fright. A jungle cat, or civet cat as they are called, had come in to my tent – the tent flap is always open for air – and was trying to get onto my bed. I suppose he could smell the warm blankets or something, but luckily my net was well tucked in all around. The only thing I could think about was to hit it with a pillow – stopping inside the net of course! After a couple of sloshes he disappeared through the tent flap and that was that. I got out and lit my hurricane lamp and had a look around but everything was OK except some apples that had been on the table. A civet cat is a little bigger than a big English cat, but with very sharp teeth and claws. They have long fur and a big bushy tail and their heads are rather like a dog's with a pointed nose. Ever since that night I've kept a large stick by my bed in case I need it for a similar occasion.

Training goes on from day-to-day in the depot and as soon as recruits are passed fit they go off in drafts to our active Battalions. The language is, of course, the main thing for me at the moment. Officers are continually coming in from the OTCs so we see a fair amount of fellows. I met a chap I was at Shrewsbury with who has come to the Gurkhas and another who lived in Herefordshire and knew uncle Jack and Auntie Ida.

It's always amazing how small the world is. Wherever I go I seem to meet somebody who knows a member of the family or has lived in Shropshire and heard of the famous *R. Gwynne & Sons*.

I am glad you got a letter from Margaret Black of Cape Town. I often wondered whether or not she would write. I thought it was better than me putting it in a letter or cable to be censored. We had four days ashore and really had a marvellous time. I must say the South Africans went right out of the way to make us welcome and feel at home and it was such a relief after being on board for so long. It's really not right to talk about that sort of thing even now so I will say no more – careless talk etc.!

I wrote about fifteen AGs from hospital – I hope to be getting a letter from home shortly, it's been six weeks at least now. It's a great event here as we are all in the same position and whenever one appears on the letter rack in the Mess, everyone rushes in to see who it is for.

There has been a break in the road between here and the railhead lately. These mountain roads often collapse during the rains, either washed away or a landslide comes down on to it from above and it takes up to a week to repair.

P.S. just got Dad's letter number 13 dated June 13th so a gap between number 3 and 13 now.

29 August 1942
Aerograph

I have just got back from six days sick leave, which I spent in Lahore with two fellows who used to be in the KSLI with me. I bumped into them quite by chance the first evening I was there. I am quite fit again and anxious to get back to work. I got a grand surprise when I got back here – there were twelve of your letters waiting for me and two AGs. Glad to hear Babs is settling in well to her new job, it will be very interesting for her in the factory. Thank you for the two photos. I could hardly recognise Robert sitting on Betty's knee. Lena and Michael also looked fit after their trip to Borth, I suppose. It's grand to know you are all well at home and that the office is going as well as possible, Dad.

Hiking in the Kangra Valley - On the top at last! 10,000 ft up it took us six hours to get up and 8 to come down again, the last three in darkness.

3 September 1942

10th GR c/o Lloyds Bank, Bombay.

Dear Mum and Dad,

I hope this reaches you safely as it has the photos enclosed which I promised. There are so many things I want to have snaps of so that you can see them later, but at the moment I have no camera. As I told you in my AG, when I got back from my sick leave I found twelve letters waiting for me. I think I have had all of the back numbers now. Leslie says his letters are coming through fairly well. I've had two letters from him lately and he seems to be having a good time in his new job. Haven't heard from Norman for about three weeks. I expect he is pretty busy. Today we have got a day's leave as it is one of the Gurkha festivals known as Janmashtami Puja.[12]

There are several during the year, each one for a different thing and in October we have the main one which is the Festival of Sacrifice lasting ten days when they worship one of the big gods, the God of Destruction.[13]

I am taking the Urdu exam on Monday although I don't think I shall pass as I have missed so much lately. That fourteen days in hospital rather put me back and I have not had time to do much since then.

I have been made Transport Officer for the Regimental Centre – I was assistant TO before but I've got the job properly now. It may mean that I shall get my Captaincy back but of course I cannot be certain. The fellow who has just finished a job was a Captain.

---

12 A festival marking Krishna's birthday, usually a day of fasting.
13 Festival of Dashera or Dashain – see letter of 13/11/42. Dasehera or Dashin, celebrates the ultimate triumph of good over evil in the form of the victory of the Goddess Durga over the demon Mahesur.

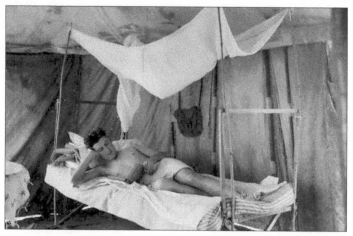

Learning Gurkhali grammar! Note the mosquito net up above – at night the sides come down and tuck under the mattress. From the head of the bed to the tent pole on the right is just under ½ the length and from the side wall behind me to the table is about ½ the width.

17 September 1942
Aerograph

Your letters and aerographs make a lot of difference and cheer me up a lot. I hear often from Leslie and Norman. They are both well and say they have a lot of work.

I am very fit now and feel as good as new after my sick leave. I took the Urdu language exam last week. I passed the oral test, but have not had the written results yet. I am teaching my orderly a bit of English. In the morning he comes in, lifts up my mosquito net and bawls 'Good morning, Sahib!' without waking me up first! The rain is almost over now – just an occasional shower. Ask Betty and Dorrie to send a family group snap.

30 September 1942

Telegram – Alhilal, Kangra Valley.

Passed language. Receiving letters Aerographs. Writing often. Love.

---

30 September 1942

Aerograph

It is good to know you are all well. I am also and quite my old self again. I sent a cable yesterday saying I had passed the Urdu language exam and have now started Gurkhali – Tell that to Old Broadbent, eh![14] The monsoon is over and the weather is glorious up here in the hills. Did you get the photos I sent by airmail?

P.S. my Captaincy came through today.

---

14 HG Broadbent, Housemaster of Moser's, Shrewsbury School from 1933-38 and had the misfortune of being Dennis's Housemaster.

4 October 1942

10 GR, from Capt DH Gwynne Camp Alhilal, Kangra Valley

Dear Mum and Dad,

The correspondence from home has been simply rolling in lately. Betty and Dorrie have written but not Lena and Madge.

It means a lot to have got my Captaincy back as we can't get either promotion or leave without it. I'm looking forward to some leave probably around Christmas. I don't know yet where I shall go – both Les and Norman are so far away now that it would take five or six days to reach either of them and I shall only be getting three weeks leave at the most. Leave out here is very different to home – you don't get seven days every three months but longer periods much less frequently. The distances are always so great that seven days leave wouldn't be much as it would be used up in travelling.

You say in one of your letters, Mum, that you couldn't find Alhilal on the map – well it's so small it probably isn't marked but if you look at the NE of Punjab you can probably find Lahore and we are about 200 miles NE again up in the foothills of the Himalaya Mountains. Actually, as the crow flies, we are only about 100 miles from the border of Tibet.

The weather up here is simply wonderful now the monsoon is over. It's about the same as an ordinary English summer and nice and cool at night. Of course, we do get days when it's absolutely scorching, but they are quite few and far between now and will be until the hot weather starts again. Everything is beautifully green after the rains and the only real trouble are mosquitoes. It is rather a bad spot for them and consequently we get a lot of malaria. It is almost unavoidable and a normal dose usually last ten to fourteen days. About the only protection you can take is to make sure that your net is fixed up properly at night so they can't get in and bite you. So far, I have managed to avoid it which is all to the good as I missed quite a lot of duty when I was in the hospital with dysentery. It's quite a business keeping fit out here because the climate is against you all the time. I hope everyone is well at home and that the children are growing up OK. It will be very interesting to see them when I come home, I wonder if they will remember me at all.

I'm glad you were able to get Alan's address. I have written him an AG today I will be writing him a proper letter later. Do you ever see Ted Robinson now? I have written several AGs to him but have had no reply yet. It was very good to see the cuttings about Simpson, Dad, and I passed them to Les. How is Frank Blakemore now

– is he out of hospital yet? I have written to the old Battalion twice, but I don't expect Frank would hear of it because both letters were to the Officers' Mess.[15] Glad to hear Stan Corbett calls now and again. There is nothing I want out here thank you, Dad. Everything is fine and my pay is coming through, also I shall be getting a bit more now for my third pip. A Captain's pay is Rs.600 a month which is about £45 pounds so I'm not doing bad am I?

On a shooting trip. Taken at about 8,000ft getting warm and sticky – we found the jungle very thick up here, with only few clearings like this one.

---

15 There is a record of a Private F. Blakemore in D Company 4 KSLI between 1939-1943 – maybe this in the same Frank Blakemore and it would certainly fit the facts as to why a letter to the 4 KSLI mess wouldn't have been forwarded on?

I expect this will be the last letter to get home before Christmas so I wish all the family as happy a Christmas as possible under the circumstances and hope we should be together again for Christmas 1943.

14 October 1942
Camp Ahilal, Kangra Valley Punjab

Dear Mum and Dad,

Was very relieved to get your mail today saying the parcel had arrived safely – I was beginning to think the fishes might be wearing the things by now. I hope you will find them OK, Mum. I can vouch they are genuine hand done as I saw others exactly the same being made on the premises. It was an amazing business altogether. I was in the bazaar and a man came up to me and said "Would your honour please follow me as I have some nice things to show you," all this in Urdu of course. Anyway, he took me to a dirty little hovel smelling chiefly of cow dung, of which most native houses are made. They also use it for fuel on the fires and smoke it instead of tobacco. And then the fun started. "Will your honour be seated," so his honour sat down and he bought out dozens of these garments. They really were a marvellous sight. I don't think you would see anything like them in England. When I had picked mine we then started arguing about the price and after about three quarters of an hour, during which I started to walk out twice when the price suddenly dropped another Rs.10 each time, eventually I got it down to what I thought was reasonable – in England it would sound ridiculously low – and then clinched the deal. After a lot more "Your honouring" and "Salaams" and "will Sahib please tell his friends" I got away. Someday I will tell you what I eventually gave after about an hour's argument standing in the middle of the bazaar!

All shopping isn't like that, of course, but this was in the proper native quarter. In any reasonably large town there is the ordinary bazaar, where you can get all the usual things, and then there is the native bazaar, where you don't go much because of the dirt and the smell and the general look of the place. Up here there are only villages, which have little stores on either side of one street, but even so you can get most things. In the cities, of course, the shops are much more European and civilized and they speak English, which is a change.

The only trouble with places like Mhow is that the place is so full of beggars who pester you the whole time, walking along with you bowing and scraping and asking for "Backshees" (money or anything you don't want). Some of the sights you see are really horrible.

They purposely cripple their children so that when they grow up, they can be professional beggars. Anyway, enough of this sordid business.

It's going to be funny here at Christmas, with the temperature about 90° in the shade, although we can see plenty of snow higher up in the mountains. They say the snow will gradually come lower and we might get some in the camp here. I'm hoping to go shooting later on. The snow drives the animals down and we should have some good sport. I have been out once since being up here – we actually saw a leopard but didn't get him. There are plenty of panther, bear and wild pig about here.

We had a panther in the camp one night but nobody felt like going after it in the dark. It's rather weird sometimes, lying in bed and listening to the jungle noises, jackals by the hundred howling all night long, an occasional panther growling about looking for a dog or a cow that hasn't been shut up and always plenty of great big bull frogs croaking like a Midland red bus blowing it's horn.

The natives bring their cattle in to their homes at night and then the people just sleep where there is a bit of space – a bit smelly but it is better than losing a cow or a bullock, which is absolutely their all. If a man has got a cow or a buffalo it means he can work, if not he has to beg. In the hills they are all land workers and their cow, or whatever they have, pulls the plough. By the way, the women do all the work while the men sit around and smoke their cow dung pipes. In the evening, the women come in from the fields, cook the evening meal, which is rice and a sort of bread pancake, and when the men have had enough, only then are the women allowed to sit down to have theirs. The same with the morning meal – they only have two meals each day, morning and evening, being exactly the same – rice and chapatti and occasionally some mutton.

Being Hindus up here, they are not allowed beef or even to kill a cow. Every village has its own Holy Bull, which is allowed to do exactly as it pleases. It can wander anywhere and even eat what it fancies on the stalls in the village – nobody dares stop it. The Holy Bull from our local village came into camp one day and got a large kick on its holy behind and was shifted out in double quick time!! The Gurkhas, although being Hindu, despise all Indians and think their beliefs are all a lot of 'hooey', which they are.

I hear from Norman and Les quite a lot. They are now, of course, a long way off from me. I haven't seen Norman at all yet. If I can manage it at Christmas, I might go down to Salem and stay with Norman.[16] Another place I should like to visit, amongst many others, is Poona – I must be able to say "when I was in Poona in '42!"

I was very pleased to hear about the Simpson case and also about Reg's Police Court work. Have you had any news of Spuddy Wood? It must be an awful blow to Marjorie. We hear the news about the sweeps over France. It seems that it must come to them all in turn, I only wish the army could have its chance, we seem to have done so little so far.

I am on the list to be drafted and shall be good and ready for it when the time comes – after waiting so long I shall take the first opportunity I get. I know you wouldn't want me to stand back at all. The Gurkhas already have a fine record in Libya and Burma. I'm only too thankful I wasn't posted to an Indian regiment, knowing now what these chaps are like.

15 October 1942
Telegram –Alhilal

Glad to hear parcel arrived Happy Birthday

---

16 A city in Tamil Nadu, Southern India, a mere 1,800 miles away!

7 November 1942

Postcard

Dear Mum and Dad,

What do you think of the news lately? It sounds pretty good, I only hope we can keep it up. I have got a wireless myself now and listen to the forces' broadcasts in my tent.

I haven't made any more arrangements about leave. I don't like to leave a comparatively new job so soon for fear something should go wrong. By the way has the Law Society said anything more about my articles? They will expire in November 1943.[17] We had the chance the other day of signing on for a Permanent Regular Commission after the war, but I turned it down. I shall have had quite enough when this is all over, I think.

All the best for Christmas and 1943.

---

17 Prior to the Second World War, articled clerks were typically indentured to their Principals for up to five years. Clerks also had to pay a Principal's premium 300 guineas as well as pay stamp duty of £80 on their articles.

After the 1914-18 War, time spent in military service counted towards the overall period of articles to be served, under the Solicitors (Articled Clerks) Act of 1918. It may be that DHG was concerned to know that the same exemption would be allowed for his military service. There was no exemption, however from taking the Law Society finals exam.

13 November 1942

Camp Achilal, Kangra Valley, Punjab

Dear Mum and Dad,

Photos enclosed which will not be of interest to the censor. The other snaps are in an album and will be an interesting record of my trip out here – we shall have to keep it in the lounge with the holiday albums!

We have just finished the two festivals which end the Gurkha year – for them I suppose it's 1943. The first was Dashera which lasted five days and the other Darwali – three days. Dashera – is their really big festival of the year which lasts certainly ten days and usually more in Nepal.[18] The two main events were the big parade for 'driving out the devils' in order to let their own gods have a free hand in the proceedings, and then the head cutting ceremony of which I was lucky enough to get some rather good snaps. The 'driving out of the devils' consists of every man turning out in native dress, if he's got any, otherwise army dress. They parade around camp shouting their war cries to drive away any devils, they even come and yell in your tent – which I thought was a bit funny, but then there might been one messing about under my bed or somewhere!

18 Dashera is more usually known as Dashain, this is the main Hindu festival in Nepal usually celebrated Sept-Oct).

Anyway, when that is done, they can start to celebrate and most of that is done with Gurkha Rum, which is about 80% neat alcohol by the taste of it. On the second night at midnight, we were invited to watch their dances being done, all in native costume, and they were extremely good. Then, on the third morning we all saw the head cutting ceremony. Five buffaloes, goats, sheep and ducks, and more or less anything, were brought into the holy circle tied to the post in the middle then beheaded. It really was a wonderful sight and certainly a very bloody one, done with a Kukri which is a short of short sword which every Gurkha – in the army or not – carries with him. They are only allowed one swipe per animal. If they can't manage it in one, they are considered very poor specimens and have brought bad luck to everyone concerned. I'm glad to say nobody brought us any bad luck this year – they were all whipped off as easy as chopping a match stick with an axe! The best snap I have is of a buffalo standing with its head hitting the ground, taken a second before it fell down. There seems to be no limit to the number of animals they slaughtered and, of course, the following night, all night, there was a colossal feast to eat them all up. Goat meat tastes nice but when you are faced with a whole goat for yourself, it's not quite so good. All the officers are asked to attend the feasts and it's always an all-night thing, if you don't peg out half way. On the sixth morning, when it was all over, they were quite normal again and ready for anything as usual.

The second one, Darwali, is merely a gambling festival, when gambling is permitted from dawn to dusk in the lines for three days and nights solidly.[19] Here, they are only allowed to gamble for money in camp, whereas in Nepal they stake anything they have got including their wives!!

I've just had my evening bath standing in a tin about the size of a large tray, and am writing this in my tent sitting in pyjamas.

How do you like the news lately? We have just heard the broadcast about the Americans, which is heartening at this end, I expect at home as well, and also hastens the day when we shall all be coming home again.

---

19 Dennis is probably referring to Tihar, the second most important Gurkhali festival after Dashain, and part of the longer five day Diwali festival itself.

My tent at Camp Achilal. Note the writing desk where all your letters are written !! Quite comfortable, but very hot during the day – the patch of sunlight (bottom left) and the view outside the door give some idea of the heat – about 120 in the shade when this was taken.

It was heartening news indeed. In November 1942, US troops entered the war in Europe in a joint Anglo-American invasion of French North Africa.

The siege of Malta was lifted on 11 November and, two days later, the 8th Army recaptured Tobruk.

Meanwhile, in Stalingrad, determined Russian resistance, extended lines of supply and the onset of the harsh Russian winter began to take their toll on German forces. The Soviet Red Army launched a counter-offensive and, on 22 November, the German 6th Army was encircled leading to its ultimate surrender.

20 November 1942
Postcard c/o Lloyds Bombay

Christmas is not a holiday for the men (not being Christians), but I have no doubt we shall have a turkey in the Mess.

I had a grand letter from Dorrie this week – with some typically Dorrie remarks – and I had a good laugh over it. There's a good programme on tonight from America, rather like the old Saturday night one at home – which we get as well – it is grand listening to the home broadcasts.

18 December 1942
Postcard – 10th Gurkha Rifles, Number 6 Advance Base, India.

I have been posted to 1st Battalion – when writing though, always use the Lloyd Bombay address.

I shall be thinking of you on 25th. I don't know where I shall be on Christmas Day – I will be in the jungle, somewhere. There's not much to say about my move, except I'm very pleased with it. I was getting a bit fed up with the Centre and am glad to be with a Battalion at last, though letters may not be as plentiful as before. Keep smiling, love to you both.

25 December 1942

Postcard – Christmas Day.

I had to revert to Lieutenant on joining the Battalion, having given up the job of MTO. My new address is number 6 Advance Base.

I have been with 1st Battalion for a month and am more or less getting down to the real thing at last. I am spending Christmas Day somewhere in the jungle and believe me it *is* jungle. There is not much of the Christmas spirit about the thing at all and it is very hard in this climate to imagine that it is December. I have been thinking about you all this morning, wondering if you have had any of the traditional snow? I am writing to Les and Norman today. I haven't heard from either of them lately.

You will realise that I am pretty busy and letters may not be as frequent now as they were before. Best wishes for 1943.

1943

Having participated in an arduous fighting retreat against tactically superior Japanese forces after the fall of Rangoon in March 1942, The Indian 17 Division, including 1/10 Gurkha Rifles, became part of IV Corps headquartered at Imphal.

1/10 GR moved from Kohima to Imphal on 1 January 1943 and then deployed to a camp along the Tiddim Road at Milestone 45. They were deployed in the Tiddim area of Burma (approximately 150 miles south of Imphal) for most of 1943 where they engaged in a series of limited offensive operations.

Deployed as a lightly armed, mobile force supported by mountain artillery, and with mules and Jeeps for transport, 1/10 GR's focus was on aggressive patrolling, which was seen as an important exercise in rebuilding confidence and raising morale after the defeat of 1942. Their role was also to act as a diversion in support of the two main operations in Burma in 1943 – the Arkan offensive (December 1942-May 1943) and the first Chindit Expedition of 1943.

The Tiddim Road, which ran from Imphal in NE India, via Tuitum on the Manipur River, to Tiddim in Chin State, Western Burma, was over 165 miles long in total. The road the was a key supply route and the main axis for deployment, advance and withdrawal by both British and Japanese forces in the Burma campaign between 1942-45.

Map of E India & Burma with Imphal - Tiddim sector highlighted

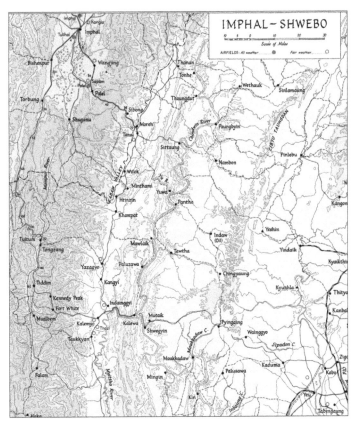

Imphal/ Tiddim/ Schewbo Sector - with the Tiddim Road
running south from Imphal via Bisehnpur, Torbung, Tuitum and
Tongzang to Tiddim at milestone 162

*125 miles of the road ran through mountainous terrain,
rising from the vast Imphal planes to breath-taking mountain peaks with elevations up to 9,000ft. One particular part
of the road between Tiddim and the Manipur River, was
known as 'the Chocolate Staircase'. In just seven miles the*

road climbed 3,000ft with thirty eight hairpin bends and an average elevation of 1 in 12 – often ankle deep in mud during the rainy season and prone to frequent landslides.

Due to its unforgiving terrain, too narrow for 3 tonners and precarious in bad weather, it was only in May 1943 that a vehicle first successfully managed to travel the whole road from Imphal to Tiddim.

7 January 1943
Postcard – c/o Lloyds Bombay.

Christmas and New Year have come and gone. I am thinking of home and remembering the old Christmases we used to have. Here's hoping next time is a real old time one. Managed to obtain a goose, but otherwise like any other day.

10 January 1943
Aerograph – Lloyds, Bombay.

Your parcel arrived today, just been opening it, found everything intact – even the bulb in the torch. Good to read the old Wellington Journal again. Not much news to tell. Fit and well. Moved again and will be off from here in a few days' time. We seem to be on the move continually now.

13 January 1943

Aerograph – No 6 Advance Base.

Parcel arrived recently, finding all the things very useful, cannot get many things now that were plentiful before we moved. Unlucky with mail lately. Camera still being repaired. Climate very reasonable.

27 January 1943

Postcard – No 6 Advance Base.

Sent you a cable on 20th saying that everything was OK. No mail for the last five weeks, I don't know what Lloyds are playing at. I am very fit, eating like a horse in fact. Difficult to write an AG as we can't get writing paper, but we do get plenty of oranges. Many of the villages we come to are empty, the natives having fled to safer parts further back. We have a Field PO which moves with us. Heard that Dr Brown of Dawley is now in Bangalore. Any news of Alan Benson?

27 January 1943

Postcard – No 6 Advance Base.

No mail for six weeks, now a batch this morning. I had a good laugh as usual over Dorrie's letter, best remarks were "Nothing happening here, Margaret Addison is not married yet but lots of people are having babies," and "Mrs Edwards from the Manor fell out of a plum tree."

Cold season nearly over, waiting for the rains to come in another month or so – won't be much fun in the jungle, everything takes longer to dry – sun still very powerful between downpours, but when you can't see the sky above you for jungle, you forget it is there.

How are you getting on at the office? I will be glad when this is over and I can come back to make another start. I wonder when that will be, though.

News heartening lately, though our front doesn't get much of a mention.

12 February 1943
Postcard – No 6 Advance Base.

Mail coming through again after seven weeks without a single word. Les and Norman have been in Bombay for fourteen days – some people get all the plums. Apart from eight days sick leave, I haven't had anything for just under a year.

21 February 1943
Telegram – Sans Origine

Fit and well. Receiving mail. Writing regularly. Love

---

26 February 1943
Aerograph – c/o Lloyds Bank, Bombay

We have been ordered not to use Adv base 6 as a postal address any more. Feeling really fit and looking very brown, I think violent exercise has had a good effect on me – have never felt quite so tough before.

Les sends me up some cigs when he can get away from Calcutta – we only have ten a week issued, they are called 'Victory Vs' and taste like bus drivers' gloves. We get tobacco issued as well so I supplement my issue with a pipe.

Grub is chiefly bully beef and biscuits with a (some-times) daily issue of rum.[1] It's a bit hard thinking of

---

1 In Field Marshall Slim's memoir "Defeat into Victory" he specifically mentions that supplying fresh meat in 1942/3 was a major logistical problem and that "Bully beef...is monotonous and very unattractive in hot weather." Bully, or corned beef, is the name given to salt cured brisket of beef preserved in gelatine. It was tinned and accompanied by hard tack biscuits. Bully beef was the staple diet of the British Army from the Boer War onwards, although not for the Indian Army for religious reasons. The term bully is thought to derive from the French word 'bouilli' or boiled.

Les and Norman in Bombay on leave, but no doubt my time will come and I shall make up for it in style.

How's the food situation at home? Keep something by for that celebration when the three of us get back. We talk an awful lot about Blighty and what we are all going to do when this is over. All I want to do is get started in the office and give you and Reg a rest. Have heard from Alan – he's chasing Rommel.

Field Marshall Erwin Rommel's Afrika Korps had been under pressure since the second battle of El Alamein in October 1942. With the Anglo-US landings in Morocco and Tunisia in early November, and the capture of Tobruk, the signs were that defeat for the 'Desert Fox' at the hands of Allied forces in North Africa was only a matter of time.

In March 1943, the British 8th Army reached the Tunisian border. Rommel returned to Germany for health reasons, and by 13 May, Axis forces in N Africa surrendered, yielding over 275,000 POWs.

2 March 1943
Airmail – c/o Lloyds Bank, Bombay

Just managed to get hold of two of these AM letters, written the other to Reg and Vera. How is everything at home? You say Wellington seems much the same, although I expect there are hundreds of strange faces about.

One of Lena's letters to Norman got sent to me here by mistake. Letter from Babs saying she was settling down in the WAAF and was being drilled by an RAF Corporal – I expect she will get on well like she does with everything she has a go at. I told her I hoped she would get a commission then we should have a Pilot Officer Gwynne to add to the list!

The last six weeks have been a good enough test for anyone, I think, but I expect we shall have to carry on a bit longer yet.

I am at the bottom of the list [**for leave**] as I was the last new officer to join before we started this spot of fun and games. At last I got some sense out of the army Pay Office – I have to pay back from 17th March [DHG's embarkation date] to the end of the year – which amounts to 2000 Rupees but I have the money in the bank –not having the chance of spending a penny at the moment.

I suppose you never hear from Hilda now, do you? I often wish I still did. [2]

---

2   DHG had a long-term girlfriend before he went overseas, he apparently broke it off at some stage before he was mobilised. This must be Hilda given later references in correspondence.

20 March 1943

Dear Mum and Dad,

Just got AG from Dad dated 12/2 - quite a quick one considering it usually takes about 10 days to get across India from Bombay. Sorry you haven't been getting mail regularly, we were told a few weeks ago that quite a bit of homebound mail was lost so I expect that would explain it. Been writing once a week which is about all I can manage. Amazing how much I miss normal things like tables and chairs which were always taken for granted before. Your bed under a tree is your sole possession, actually my bed is a valise containing two blankets and a spare shirt or two. I dumped all my kit back at base as we are only allowed 12 lbs of stuff in weight, luxuries have gone. Weather breaking a bit, monsoon will soon be here.

Wrote to Norman about three weeks ago when he was in Kakul on a course, but have had no reply.[3] I hope to go on leave in August or September, I will get ten days plus travel to wherever I decide to go. I shall have to pass through Calcutta so hoping to see Les both going and coming back. Might go to Kashmir.

---

3   Kakul is located in modern day Pakistan and is today the location of the Pakistan Military Academy. ANG was on a course in Kakul at this time prior to being promoted to Major.

4 April 1943
Airmail

Got your AG saying OD had passed on [Murphy, Lena Gwynne's Uncle] please say something to Ron [his son] when you next see him.

Will be glad to get a snap of Babs in her uniform – tell her she must get up to at least a Squadron Leader! Had letter from Dorrie last week saying John was in the Home Guard.

News is very scarce here, we just keep on day after day, longing for the day we can get on the boat for home. Wouldn't it be grand if all three of us could get on the same boat? I often think of the time when I shall see old England again and searching the dockside for you to meet me there.

Still waiting to hear about leave. I don't know where Norman is at the moment. Sorry haven't sent any more snaps, but no camera.

22 April 1943
Airmail

News scarce as the rains have begun again, slowed up as impossible to do much and Malaria gets very bad as well. A small dose usually lasts 2-3 days, high temperature and you feel generally run down.[4] Try to keep you posted as much as possible, but of course very difficult to say anything which will get past the censors. I don't expect you know where I am but expect you may get some clue to it from the wireless news sometime. We go weeks without hearing anything from the outside world or any of the other war fronts. My leave is getting nearer, in about four months in August at height of the monsoon, so I will have to choose between a hot one [the plains] or a wet one [higher up]: what would you do, chums?

26 April 1943
Airmail

Three letters just came through for me – my AG home got through in fourteen days, certainly a record. Not much news, restricted as to what I can say. Written to congratulate Stanley [Corbett] on his marriage – he would probably have asked me to be a groomsman or something like that. Written to Dorrie and John today, let me know as soon as possible after the baby is born what it is (i.e. nephew or niece).

Back at the moment on a bit of a rest, so have been

---

4   Slim estimated that for every man evacuated wounded in 1943, 120 men were evacuated sick and that malaria rates amongst troops was 84% per annum, with dysentery being the next in terms of rates of incidence. At one stage evacuations rose to over 12,000 per day.

trying to get off some letters. Weather terrifically hot and raining as well – monsoon opening up. Strange to compare it with the English weather where you never know if it is going to be wet or fine – and here where you know for certain that until the monsoon comes it won't rain and as soon as it ends it won't rain again for another eight months.

Glad to hear Law Society are making provisions for fellows like me – the sooner I can be back and start on it the better.

26 April 1943
Airmail – to Dorrie and John Edwards

I have had no leave since I arrived in India, except 8 days sick leave when I came out of hospital last September, but I felt too weak to do anything then (or anybody for that matter!! Eh John!!) [**Is DHG calculating that September was the month Dorrie fell pregnant? -Ed**] Which reminds me, how's my old pal Margaret Addison getting on?[5] Remember me to her when you see her will you!

On 2 May 1943, 1/10 GR moves to Shillong, an Indian hill station some 300 miles NE of Imphal for a rest period.

It is said that the rolling hills around the town re-

---

5   See Dorrie's comment about Margaret Addison in her letter of 27 January 1943.

minded the British of Scotland, and that they referred to it as the "Scotland of the East."

14 May 1943
Airmail – c/o Lloyds Bank, Bombay

Babs wrote on 9/4/43 while she was on leave, although the address was Newquay. She says it is much the same as it always was. I must say it brings back happy memories to read about Newquay. I hope you will both go down there for a bit of a holiday when you can, as I'm sure you need it.

Looking forward to leave, should be fairly soon. As I expect you know Les is leaving Calcutta, so probably won't be able to see him on my way back.

We have moved back a bit since I last wrote and are now in a rest area. I must say it wasn't until we got back here and could relax that I realised what a strain the last few months had been.

Haven't heard from Norman for a few weeks and didn't know he was a Major until you told me. Les wrote saying he was about to move again, seems to be doing very well at his job. I hope he gets a promotion. My chances at the moment are rather slight I'm afraid.

23 May 1943

Dear Mum and Dad,

At last I have managed to get something definite about my leave and will be going on Aug 26th I think. At the moment I am on a course for Coy Commanders and after that go on another course finishing Aug 20th. After regular leave every three months in Blighty, waiting fifteen months for it out here seems ages but the time goes amazingly quickly as we are always so busy. Moved out of it for a bit, now going through a period of refresher training, living in comparative civilisation again. Actually saw a picture the other day which was a novel experience, not having seen one for five months.

Glad to hear everything is going well at the office and that you are managing with the small staff. It must be difficult at times. I was very sorry to read in your last letter about Mr Latham and hope things are ok for Mrs L and the children.

Did you hear the news on the wireless about Brigadier Wingate's Brigade and expedition into Burma? I'm glad something has now been given out as it will give you some idea of what is going on and what I'm doing. I hope they let you know some of the details.

Brigadier Orde Wingate was the driving force behind the creation of the Chindits, a long-range penetration unit trained in jungle and guerrilla warfare and tasked with taking the war to the Japanese Army deep behind their own lines.

In February 1943, 3,000 Chindits crossed into Burma on a three month mission, from which only 2,182 returned. The impact that the Chindits had on the Japanese war machine on the ground in Burma is disputed, but the effect on morale of the troops in the theatre is undoubted.

Further Chindit operations followed in 1944. Wingate himself was killed in a B-25 crash on 24 March 1944 during the battle of Imphal and is buried in Arlington National Cemetery, Washington.

20 June 1943

Airmail – 6 Advance Base PO via Lloyds Bank, Bombay

Your mail and cables coming through well recently, but I'm afraid I haven't been able to reply very often. Extremely difficult to find an opportunity to sit down and write a letter, not knowing where you are going to be from day to day.

Like you, I haven't heard from Norman for about three months. I haven't heard from Les since he left Calcutta.

Betty and Robert will have enjoyed their stay at Eversleigh. Babs wrote from Cambridge saying she is getting on well and liking the work. Pity she left Newquay; I was hoping you would have gone down there for a bit of a rest.

Leave seems to have been fated from the start, and is now postponed indefinitely which probably means I won't get it at all unless I get a special grant after this job that I'm on now. Can't say any more than that.

Weather particularly bad with both monsoon and Malaria in full swing. Got over last spot of Malaria but not expecting to be entirely free – impossible to miss it completely.

Hundreds of things to tell you about but which will have to keep. Perhaps you hear some of them on the wireless – going to take ages to tell you everything when we get home.

Remember me to all the folks who ask after me – Keep Smiling.

23 June 1943
Telegram

Everything going well. Receiving mail. Writing as often as possible. Love.

There is also a handwritten note from RG to DHG on the bottom of this telegram, saying 'Nothing heard from Nor-

man for four months, can you tell us anything or make enquiry. Love Mother & Dad.'

In July 1943, 1/10 GR is moved back to the Tiddim sector in the Kennedy Peak - Fort White area in the Chin Hills. Kennedy Peak at 8,800ft is the highest point of the Tiddim-Kalewa Road.

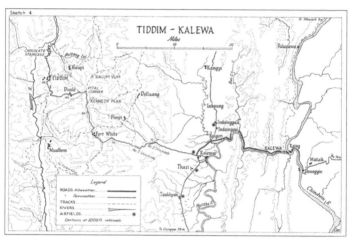

Map of Tiddim to Fort White Sector, East of the Manipur River

4 July 1943

Airmail – 6 Advance Base PO via Lloyds Bombay

Mail has just come up and I've been lucky again – grand to see your letters come rolling in and to sit down in a quiet spot and read all the home news.

Sorry you haven't heard from Norman, Les hasn't either. I can't think why he hasn't written but I'm sure there is no need for you to worry. He may have been sent out on a job where he cannot get any mail back, but will be doing so as soon as he finishes the particular job.

We are now back in the fray and we often wonder how much you manage to hear at home. The wireless out here – so we are told – gives out quite a lot of news about this front, which should be interesting for you at home.

Got the two snaps of Robert. I must say I wouldn't have recognised him if you hadn't written his name on the back! Don't tell Betty that!

I'm sorry to read that you don't think you will be taking a holiday this summer – I think you ought to if you get a chance and I've told Babs to try to persuade you both.

AG news from others this week – Frank Sharpe now a Captain in N Africa somewhere. I am of course still a Lieutenant and likely to remain as such until the end of the war as far as I can see – what a life!

14 July 1943
Airmail

The weather is very wet and we are very lucky if we are ever dry. Usually I manage to keep my spare trousers and shirt more or less dry for sleeping in but my blanket is always sodden, as it is practically impossible to find a dry patch of ground to sleep on. Look forward to when it is all over – a pair of pyjamas and a real bed to sleep in!!!

Sorry to hear you still haven't heard from Norman and I cannot understand why – Les also says he hasn't heard for some months. I'm making all the enquiries I can – remember I'm not even in India now. Please don't worry though, I'm sure he will write soon – he has probably been in hospital with Malaria or something. It must be very worrying for you and Lena – but look on the bright side, I'm sure he is perfectly OK.

We have just heard the grand news about Sicily. Someday I hope they tell you something of what we have been doing on this front. I wish I could tell you myself, but will keep it all for when I come home.

After defeating Italy and Germany in the North African Campaign, the United States and Great Britain, the leading Allied powers, looked ahead to the invasion of occupied Europe and the final defeat of Nazi Germany. The Allies de-

cided to move next against Italy, hoping an Allied invasion would remove that fascist regime from the war, secure the central Mediterranean and divert German divisions from the northwest coast of France and from the Eastern Front.

The Allied invasion of Sicily, codenamed Operation Husky, commenced on the night of the 9 July with amphibious and airborne landings and was successfully concluded by 17 August.

The immediate impact was to re-open the Mediterranean shipping lanes to merchant shipping for the first time since 1941 and to cause the downfall of Benito Mussolini.

Hitler was also forced to cancel a major offensive at Kursk on the Eastern front and divert troops to Italy and the Balkans.

Around one fifth of the German army was eventually diverted from the East to Southern Europe as Italy was knocked out of the war.

30 July 1943
Airmail - c/o Lloyds Bank, Bombay

Your letter number 65 of June 12th has just arrived and also one from you, Mum. Nothing from Norman – it's certainly very strange. I'm sure he is quite OK, he has probably been sent on a long move somewhere and has been unable to get any mail through.

I'm glad you managed to hear about the Wingate expedition and you will know where I am and something of what I have been doing – and we are certainly doing plenty. We were hoping to get relieved but apparently it wasn't possible and we're still in it. Still we're getting something done now and the Japs certainly aren't having things all their own way.

I wrote to Barbara in her new station in Surrey, have enquired about sending some money home for war savings etc. Being up here so long my bank balance is steadily rising – good thing to send a little home each month out of my pay so it won't decrease the capital but the income will be less (that sounds like a good one!!).

2 August 1943
Airmail

Well Aug 2nd is here again and my best birthday present so far is that I have my Captaincy back with effect from yesterday. Extra pay will come in useful. I have written to Les asking him to send a cable for me as I am nowhere near a Post Office.

On 5/6 August 1943, 1/10 GR are involved in an unsuccessful operation to take Basha Hill in the Kennedy Peak sector from a well dug in enemy force, losing the commander of 'B' Company in the attempt. DHG now takes

over command of 'B' Company, even though he was rela-
tively new in the Battalion.

13 August 1943
Airmail

I didn't go on the course in the end as the CO couldn't spare me from the Battalion at that time, so my chances of seeing a bit of civilisation again were squashed – also the leave which, as you know, never came off.

Am feeling a bit tired these last few days, having just come back from another show in which we had quite a bit of fun – maybe you will be hearing something about it soon.

I hear from Les quite frequently, he seems to have got over his jaundice now. I passed him a *Journal* which you sent me, in which I read all about Mr Latham. It was grand reading the local news again –it was the first *Journal* I have read since leaving home eighteen months ago.

Hope Dorrie and Peter are doing well – I expect they will be back home by now. No news of Norman, I'm afraid. Give my love to Lena and Madge and the others.

In mid-August 1943, 1/10 GR is relieved and returns to camp in the Tuitum area around Milestone 132 on the Tiddim Road. On 24 August, the Battalion receives a message of thanks for its recent efforts from the 17 Div Commander Maj. General 'Punch' Cowan.

3 September 1943
Airmail

Four years of war today and I'm beginning to feel quite a veteran having served a total of four and a half years. Let's hope it will soon be over and that we can all get back to normal lives and jobs again. My articles are up next month and I have only served six months of them, really. I got a letter from Les saying he had not heard again from Norman since the telegram saying "am alright – letter following". Am very anxious to hear what he has been up to all this time.

Still looking forward to some leave, I wonder what the chaps in Blighty would say if they had to wait as long as we do for it. If only we were near civilisation – but still, we're getting on with the job here and that counts for a lot. I have just lately been doing similar things to what I told you about before and I am feeling grateful for a day or two's rest before the next.

4 September 1943

Airmail

Batch of mail just arrived - have been well rewarded for my patience. Two from Mum wishing me a Happy Birthday – I thought of home and you all a lot on that day – I hope we shall be together for yours and mine next year, Dad. Happy birthday for the 21st Dad, sorry I was a bit late for it. Letter from Les enclosing a long letter from Mum with snaps of the children which I enjoyed seeing, passed it back to Les so he can send it on to Norman.

I often wish I could have my camera, but forbidden. I've been trying to think how Eversleigh looks without the railings although you say they didn't want to try to get the Veranda ones down! I don't blame them.

Fancy you having to stand in a queue for one and a half hours for a ration book, Mum – can't you get somebody to do it for you? Les has sent parcel of magazines, we seldom see any reading materials. I've been looking out for your parcel of cigs, Dad, but they haven't turned up yet. Hope nobody at the Base has had them. News scarce, usual rumours floating about, but I'm keeping quiet until I get on a truck and really start going back. I've been had before and am expecting nothing.

By September 1944, over one million tonnes of iron gates and railings had been gathered in Britain to help with the war effort under a programme overseen by Lord Beaver-brook.

There has been much speculation around what happened to all of the iron, since it seems that no more than about twenty-five per cent of the material was ever melted down to produce ordinance and weapons.

Eversleigh House, complete with railings, taken in 1918.

Faced with an oversupply, rather than halt the collection, which had turned out to be a unifying effort for the country and of great propaganda value, the government allowed it to continue. The ironwork collected was stockpiled away from public view in depots, quarries, railway sidings. After the war, even when raw materials were still in short supply, the widely held view is that the government did not want to reveal that the sacrifice of so much highly valued ironwork had been in vain, and so it was quietly disposed of, or even buried in landfill or at sea.

10/11 September 1943

Telegram – exact date unclear, but possibly 10/11 September

Fit and well. Receiving mail. Norman okay. Love

On 7 October 1943, Admiral Lord Louis Mountbatten arrived in India to take up his appointment as Supreme Allied Commander South East Asia.

20 October 1943

Telegram

On leave together. Having grand time. Happy birthday from us both. Love to all

---

12 November 1943

Airmail

Settled down again and replying to letters found waiting. One from Norman. Good to be back at work, having been in Calcutta with Les having far too good a time. Rains are over, fairly cool by day and even cold at night. At least we can say "no more rain for six months" which is more than you can!

Wrote to Babs how good it was to see Les again and talk about you and home. It certainly renews the energy to get on with the job and be able to come back to you again and say we've finished the task and can get back to the office again. Babs has had a step up and I hope she will continue and get further promotion.

Had a letter form the Income tax at home saying I owe them £17-0-0 which they failed to deduct from my pay in 1941!! They are having it deducted out here. Keep Smiling. The news in Europe is very good isn't it.

With Mussolini deposed from power and the collapse of the fascist government, on 13 October 1943, Italy declared war on its former Axis partner Germany and joined the battle on the side of the Allies.

On 6 November, 1943 the Red Army liberated Kiev on the Eastern front.

14 November 1943
Airmail

I don't know if this will get to you before Christmas, but wish you all at home a happy a time as possible. I expect that like last year it will be quite quiet, but you will be having the girls calling in with Reg and Vera. I sincerely hope that next year will be much happier and that we shall all be together again like the real old Christmases we used to have at home. Both Les and I have had letters from Norman – good to know he is OK and I hope that on my next leave I shall be able to spend it with them both. Wonder what weather you are having at home – out here it is very pleasant and nice and cool, though a bit cold at night especially with only just a blanket to wrap around yourself, but I'd rather be cold than rained on all night. Hope you get this before 25th - what price turkey and Christmas pudding this year?

19 November 1943
Airmail

Been given two of these Christmas letter cards so I am writing again to say Happy Christmas. I've just had another letter from Norman telling me about his move and his new job. He certainly has been doing extremely well lately and speaks of getting a further promotion to Lt. Colonel shortly – Lena will be very pleased if it comes off, won't she – these Gwynnes always were go ahead people! Although he says there's not much chance yet, it's all a question of vacancies not of how good the officer happens to be. The same applies to me as well and I don't see any chances yet.

I'm glad to hear that the papers at home have been showing pictures of the famine in Bengal. The sights in the street of Calcutta are really horrible and the Government seems to be doing absolutely nothing about it – except talking. But I think the right man is on the job here now – being a Military man he can do much more and knows so much more than the old Viceroy.

It really makes my blood boil to read what some of our people are saying in Parliament at home – fools who have never been near India and don't know a thing about it. The real trouble is profiteering and black market – the poor people can never have enough money to pay the lowest prices which are being asked for now. It makes you think a bit when people talk about "the gem of the British Empire" doesn't it. I could go on for hours about this – it's a thing I feel very bitter about.

Letter from Betty and John saying the harvest was all in and that John is having a very busy time etc. I expect Dorrie and John are as well. I think I told you I had finally heard from Hilda, didn't I – did you write at all? Happy Christmas and love to you both.

Lord Wavell was appointed as Viceroy of India in July 1943, to succeed the Marquess of Linlithgow, and then in September he added Governor General to his title.

One of Wavell's first actions in office was to address the Bengal famine of 1943 by ordering the army to distribute relief supplies to the starving rural Bengalis. He then attempted to increase the supply of rice in order to reduce prices.

The famine was largely man made, a toxic combination of the scorched earth tactics employed by British troops in the path of the advancing Japanese forces, the disruption of rice imports from Burma itself caused by the Japanese invasion and a cyclone that hit the rice harvest, all of which combined to cause profiteering, black marketeering and hoarding.

The Bengal famine cost between two and three million lives through starvation and Malaria. Initially, the British authorities were accused of taking advantage of war-time censorship to keep the news quiet.

Inflation and the impact of war on the economy of the region was also an issue not only for British India, but also in Japanese occupied Burma and beyond.

After the fall of Mandalay on 21 May 1942 (around the date DHG arrived in India), British forces retreated into India. As with all their newly occupied territories in SE Asia, the Japanese military authorities confiscated all local hard currency in Burma and issued their own invasion currency - known as southern Development Bank notes (or in Japanese, Greater East Asian war scrip). In the case of Burma, these were denominated in both Cents (1,5,10) and Rupees (1/4, 1/2, 1, 5 and 10). In 1944 they issued a 100 Rupee note (presumably evidence that inflation was an issue for the Japanese occupied areas too).

Japanese Invasion Currency

The letter 'B' of the notes indicted they were issued for Burma, although he also had in his possession a note marked 'M' issued for Malaya. This could have been brought with Japanese units as they moved in to Burma from Malaya.

The invasion money was cancelled and rendered obsolete at the end of the war by punching holes in it, which explains the damage to the notes themselves.

At the end of the war, the outstanding balance of Southern Development Bank scrip across Asia was estimated to be more than thirteen billion, all of which became immediately worthless. Despite post-war litigation, Japan has never paid any personal compensation to any individual whose currency was confiscated, although Japan did make restitution on a national level under the treaty of San Francisco in 1953.

Japanese Imperial Currency

DHG also had some captured Japanese imperial notes in his possession. The pictured 1 and 50 Sen (0.5 Yen) notes are actual, rather than a Military, Yen notes as they are convertible into silver. The 1-yen note seen here was in issue from 1889 to December 1942 and was convertible into 1 yen of silver. It features on the front Takenouchi no Sukune, a legendary Japanese figure who supposedly lived to be 280 years old. The 50 Sen note was issued sometime between 1938 and 1945, when it was withdrawn, and features Mount Fuji on the obverse.

The Japanese military also issued Japanese military yen in the occupied territories, typically based on the design of the yen, but with no reference to the Bank of Japan and not specifically convertible into gold or silver. They were, however, convertible into regular Japanese yen upon presentation.

10 December 1943
Airmail – c/o Lloyds, Bombay (written in pencil)

Just received my Christmas parcel, everything will be very useful, especially the mosquito cream. It was grand to read the *Journal* again and read some familiar names. I saw Sophie Banks is in it again! I also read an account of Norah's death.[6] I did write to Ron – I hope my letter was OK as I didn't quite know what to say, but Ron will understand alright. Glad you got the cables which Les and I sent from Calcutta and know now what a good time we had together. I heard from him again this week telling me that Bonnie [Leslie's Dalmatian] had had an argument with a hedgehog. I hope he is OK again now.

Sorry about pencil – out of ink at the moment. Your

---

6   Norah, wife of Ron Murphy, was crushed to death by a cow in November, 1943.

letter number 85 came the other day telling me that you had managed to have a bit of a gathering for your birthday, Mum. The calendar you sent me has been much admired by our British Officers. It has reminded us all of the same thing – home.

The 1/10 GR regimental diary signs off 1943 with the observation that "the year ended with the battalion getting well into its stride with patrol, ambush and 'Commando' activity in the forward areas, particularly about Vangte, Thukiai and Lophei, west of Fort White." Elsewhere it comments that the battalion had become famous for its series of raids, ambushes and patrols, "which made the name 'Gurkha' feared and detested by the Japanese."

1944

4 January 1944

Airmail

Many thanks for all your mail it has been coming through very well lately. Christmas and New Year are both things of the past again now. Though I was not able to celebrate them, I was thinking of you all at home and wishing that I was there with you.

Hope you are getting my mail OK. I have been writing as often as I can. I've usually managed one every week or so.

Had a letter from Lena this week also a cable from Ron. I hope Michael is better now, I know what dysentery is like, having had it twice, and can sympathise with him.

28 January 1944

Airmail – Lloyds Bank, Bombay – from Major D H Gwynne

My promotion came through a few days ago, but so far I haven't been able to send you a cable. I shall get back pay for my Majority to 1/11/43 so there will be quite a bit to come.

My total pay per month will now be roughly 700 Rupees which is just over £50!!! Had a note from the bank saying they have sent a lump sum of 1,500 Rupees to Lloyds, Wellington to be credited to your account, Dad. There seems to be no point having the money in the bank here as I can't use it and it will be better off buying Savings Certificates etc.

An officer called to see me the other day who had been working with Les in Chittagong and Les has been posted forward to near us.[1] Unfortunately, I was away on a job at the time, but am hoping to see him again sometime and ask all about Les. I hear from Norman quite often now and he seems fit and well, though very busy. From what he says he seems to be living in absolute luxury compared with me, a real bed to sleep in being the main item. Anyway, I expect the time will

---

1   Chittagong is in Bangladesh. The posting was possibly something to do with the Arkan offensive which launched in December 1942).

come soon enough as it did for me – when all things are luxuries which one took for granted before the rough stuff started.

News is very scarce. We sometimes hear the wireless news from home relayed through Delhi, but they don't say much, if anything, about our front. No doubt when the novelty of the 8th Army has worn off, people will begin to wonder what the other Armies – the 14th for instance – are doing.

DHG's observation that the 14th Army in Burma never received any news coverage was a common refrain, and led to the invention of the soubriquet 'The Forgotten Army'.

This was in large part a reflection of the prioritisation of the European and North African campaigns by the Allies from 1943-45 from a strategic perspective and in the public imagination and press from a 'good news' perspective.

The 14th Army were not alone: British forces fighting up the mountain ranges of Italy in the harsh winter of 1944 referred to themselves ironically as the 'D-Day Dodgers.'

In Dennis's papers, there is a typed song or poem entitled 'Sticking it out in Delhi' which includes the following verses:

> *Fighting the Nazis from Delhi*
> *Fighting the Japs from Kashmir*

Exiled from England, we feel you should know
The way we are taking it here

Sticking it out at the Cecil,
Doing our bit for the war...
Going through hell at Maiden's Hotel,
Where they stop serving lunch after four!'

Tightening our belts at Nirula's
Taking it all on the chin.
For the sake of the nation
We suffer privation
Just look at the shortage of gin

Having concluded the North African campaign and participated in the invasion of Sicily before moving up to mainland Italy, General Bernard Montgomery handed over command of the 8th Army to Lt Gen Oliver Leese and returned home at the end of 1943 to begin preparations for Operation Overlord.

The Desert Rats of the 8th Army who, by early 1944, were fighting on the Allied eastern flank in Italy continued to get plenty of column inches in the absence of good news elsewhere.

Progress was slow in the face of a determined German rear-guard action, and on 17 January the battle for 14th century mountain-top abbey of Monte Cassino began.

8 February 1944
Airmail

Today's mail bag brought me four letters which I was very grateful for as I haven't been getting many for a week or two. Also, your parcel of cigs hasn't yet arrived so I'm afraid it must have been in that lot which got lost. Letter from Eric Stocks from Africa. It's a long time since I heard from him, he said he had just had a month's leave in Nairobi – which is Alan Benson's home, incidentally.

I was sorry to hear about Auntie Jessie, but as you say it was a happy release for her. If you see Roy and Edna again please remember me to them. Glad Michael is better and back at school and that all the other children are doing well. I hope I will be able to recognise them when I come back. It doesn't seem two years ago this month since I came home on embarkation leave, does it?

News here pretty thin, but I am glad to see you say that you are getting news of the 14th Army now. It should be bigger and better news as time goes on.

Les and Norman are both well. I hear John Jones is now out here and is stationed in Delhi, but I don't know what sort of job he has. Did you get my cable telling you about my promotion? I know you would be very pleased about it.

15 February 1944
Telegram

Promoted Major, Receiving mail.
Am fit and well. Love

On 27 February, Dennis's Battalion was deployed to Mualbem, 10 miles South of Tiddim and 40 miles inside Burma.

From the end of February to 10ᵗʰ March, Dennis and his Company were responsible for 56 enemy killed and a definite 13 wounded in a series of attacks on Japanese forces in the area, while suffering only two casualties of his own.

2 March 1944
Postcard to Robert Gwynne, Dennis's father, from HH Hardy [Headmaster of Shrewsbury School], Kingsland house, The Schools, Shrewsbury

Thanks very much for your note about DHG having been promoted Major. I am not quite clear whether he is attached to the Gurkha Rifles or now transferred definitely. Anyhow, it is a fine regiment to be with, and he is a pretty young Major.

On 7 March 1944, the Japanese 15th Army, under General Mataguchi, launched Operation U-GO, aimed at destroying British forces at Imphal and Kohima. These battles were to be the turning point of the Burma campaign and the high-water mark of the Japanese advance on India.

Imphal, capital of the Indian state of Manipur, was a major British supply and logistics base. If Imphal was taken, the road to India would be wide open and the principal route for supply of Chang Kai-shek's Nationalist forces and their US allies in China would also be closed.

Kohima, eighty-four miles to the North of Imphal in Nagaland NE, was a key vantage point over the supply lines that ran along the Imphal/Kohima Road. If the Japanese offensive succeeded in taking the high ground overlooking the road, Imphal would be cut off.

The battle for Kohima and Imphal was later described by Lord Mountbatten as one of the greatest in history, not least because of the extremely hostile environment in which they were fought. In his report to the Combined Chiefs of Staff, he later highlighted the extreme challenges posed by both landscape and climate for troops fighting in the Burma Campaign:[2]

---

2   From Report to the Combined Chiefs of Staff by SAC South East Asia – (HMSO 1951) on Burma Campaign.

> *The Frontier is marked by a series of precipitous mountain ranges ... intersected by fast rivers running in deep valleys and generally covered with the most dense jungle. The highest mountains lie in the north where peaks reach a height of 12,000ft. In the south they rise to 3,000-4,000 ft and malaria and scrub typhus are endemic below these heights. Apart from the Tamu and Tiddim mule tracks, no form of road connecting India and Burma existed prior to 1942.*

Field Marshall Slim also emphasised the impact of topography on the ability of the troops to physically wage offensive operations against the enemy and the importance of unit cohesion, morale and strong leadership:

> *Companies, even Platoons under junior leaders, become the basic units of the jungle. Out of sight of one another, often out of touch, their wireless blanketed by hills, they marched and fought on their own, often for days at a time.*

In addition to strategic importance of Kohima to the north of Imphal, control of the 160 odd miles of the Tiddim Road to the south was also key to the defence of Imphal. The Tiddim Road was to be the setting for seven bloody and hard fought battles from March to June 1944, three in the Chin Hills and four in the Manipur plains, before the Battle of Imphal was finally won.

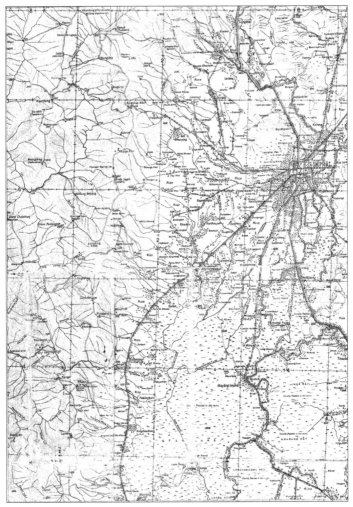

DHG's map – Imphal in NE Corner, with Tiddim Road running SW

12 March 1944

Aerograph

Found quite a pile waiting for me when I came back yesterday after being out on a job for sixteen days. Glad to hear that my cheque had been transferred to you OK and that the monthly amount had begun to arrive. You mention RG Shaw in one of your letters, I never actually met him but I passed over his stretch of road on my way to Burma and when I went back on leave.[3] I see also in the *Journal* you sent me that he has been awarded the MBE.

Letter from Alan Benson – he has been on leave to his home in Kenya, but I imagine he is now back in Italy. Norman and Les write when they can and we always pass around any home news that any of us get. Les has had another move. Sorry to hear Babs didn't pass out in her latest exam, but she has already done very well anyway, hasn't she?

I may not have time to write to her for a few days.[4] By the way, never worry if you don't hear from me for a week or two at any time. Its sometimes absolutely impossible to write letters, but I always do when I get a

3   R.G. Shaw is probably Robert Gordon Shaw, Co-founder of Shaw Wallace & Company, established in 1886 in Calcutta. The enterprise seems to have involved in the production and sale of Indian made foreign liquor, especially Royal Challenge and Director's Special Whisky.
4   DHG is possibly temporarily out of the line when he writes on 12 March, which is the 6th day of U-GO).

chance. Very fit though I feel a bit exhausted sometimes when the strain begins to tell. Uncle Will will tell you what the Burma climate can be like.[5] Looking out for your next lot of cigs which, I hope, will arrive safely.

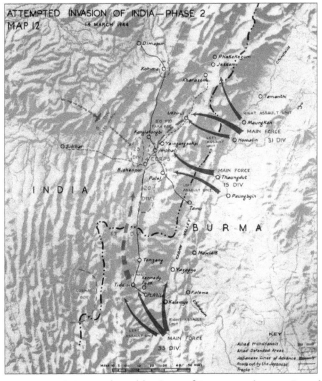

Operation U-GO March 1944 – Line of Japanese advance, British retreat (Report to the Combined Chiefs of Staff by SAC South East Asia – HMSO 1951) Burma Campaign)

---

5   Uncle Will was Willam Gwynne (RG's younger brother) who served with 4 KSLI in SE Asia from 1914-17, before the Bn was posted to France in late 1917.

Just a day after this letter was written, on 13 March, Dennis's Division was effectively cut off as Japanese forces took Tuitum Saddle, a few miles behind their positions, forcing them to withdraw towards Imphal. Holding the high ground at Tuitum was key because it dominated the Tiddim Road at the point it crossed the Manipur River bridge and wound northwards back to India and the Imphal plain.

On 15 March, the Division (including 1/10 GR) assaulted Japanese positions on the Tuitum Saddle, in an effort to force the enemy away from the Tiddim Road. Dennis's Company was in reserve for the main attack of 15 March, but successfully broke up an enemy attempt to counter-attack the rear of another Company in his Battalion.

On 16 March, Dennis led B Company on another attack on the left knoll of the Tuitum Ridge, following a creeping artillery barrage so closely that six of his men were wounded by their own shell fire, but the tactic enabled the Gurkhas to close on the Japanese positions at speed, forcing the enemy to flee in confusion.

Between 18-26 March, Dennis's men were dug in on the Tuitum Ridge overlooking the Manipur River bridge. For seven days and nights his Battalion held off repeated Japanese attacks in force, inflicting many casualties on the enemy in the process, while 17 Division crossed the river below and escaped back up the Tiddim Road towards Imphal. 1/10 Gurkha Rifles, having fought a successful rearguard action, was one of the last units to cross the Manipur River bridge, which was then blown up once they were safely over.

On 29 March, Japanese forces successfully cut the road between Imphal and Kohima at Maram, some 50 miles north of Imphal, meaning that Imphal could now only be supplied by air.

Having only recently arrived at Imphal from fighting on the Tiddim Road in Burma, on 8/9 April, Dennis's Company was soon involved in fighting at Mapao, some ten miles north of Imphal, in order to help clear the Imphal-Kohima road of enemy forces.

B Company was ordered to take the Mapao Spur, one of a series of ridges up to 5,000 ft high on which the enemy have taken up defensive positions overlooking the Imphal/Kohima road. Dennis and his men arrived at night at what they had been told was a position clear of enemy, only to find it occupied.

At dawn on 9 April, Dennis led the first of three assaults on the position, each time along a knife edge ridge which limited the number of men he could bring to bear in the attack. Each attack was met with a hail of enemy machine gun and mortar fire, and Dennis and his men were held up and driven back. By the time of the third assault, the position had been reinforced and the Gurkhas were forced to fall back and observe the enemy until Dennis's Company was ordered back to his Battalion positions.

12 April 1944
Telegram

Safe and well. Unable to write letters. Love to all

---

12 April 1944
Airmail

I find now that I can drop you a line. Everything here is ok, though life is rather hectic.

Looking forward to those cigs when they come. I heard from Leslie yesterday saying he is now back with his old unit and enjoying a bit of a rest. I told you in my telegram not to worry if you didn't hear from me for long periods – writing letters is getting very difficult, but I will write or cable as often as I can.

Very sorry to hear that you had not been well lately, Dad, and hope that you are fit again now. How did you enjoy your stay at the Buttery[6] – it would make a nice change for you both and a well needed rest. Norman wrote saying he has had another change of jobs and also got his promotion which is good news, isn't it? If only Les could get his it would make things complete. It may

---

6 John and Dorrie's farm.

be a few days before I get another chance to sit down with paper and pencil (I'm afraid I lost my pen).

20 April 1944
Airmail

Very many thanks for the cigs, the very next day another parcel arrived from Auntie Ida and Uncle Jack. They are taking a lot of looking after as everyone is very short of cigs. Several officers have asked me how I managed to get them and who his people have to write to to get them sent out. Are all mine (letters) getting through OK? We haven't heard lately that any home-going stuff has been lost so you should be getting all the ones I manage to write.

How did Frank Sharpe manage to get back home? I didn't expect him to get married yet, as far as I knew he was out in W Africa somewhere. Eric wrote again, he is in Ceylon so I might be seeing him if he sent on to the Burma front.[7]

I hope Reg is better now, sorry to hear that he had been ill again. It would mean a lot of extra work for you, Dad. By the way have you heard any more about my articles which have expired now?

---

7   Kandy, Ceylon was the location of Admiral Lord Mountbatten's HQ for SEAC.

I'm afraid I lost my letter from the Law Society you sent me. Glad you are receiving my monthly allowance; Lloyds Bank out here are very good – will be sending another lump sum in a few months when my a/c has mounted up again.

24 April 1944
Telegram

Will write soon as possible. Am okay. Receiving mail.
Don't worry about non receipt mail from me.
Much Love

In early May, 17 Division was back in the line facing the seasoned Japanese 33 Division once more on the Tiddim Road at Bishenpur, fifteen miles south west of Imphal.

Less than three miles to the south of Bishenpur on the Imphal plain was the small rural village of Potsangbam, or 'Pots and Pans' as it was known by British troops. Potsangbam was to become important because of its situation on the Tiddim Road, which passed through the village over a small road bridge.

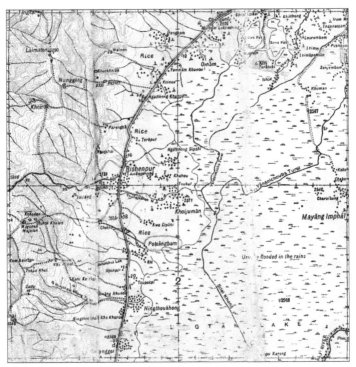

Enlargement of DHG's map – Bishenpur, Potsangbam

Enemy forces had begun to occupy the village in increasing numbers at the end of April after taking up strategic positions in the hills to the west, which meant the village was in full sight of Japanese artillery positions.

4 May 1944
Telegram

Arrival of cigarettes prevents crisis. Am fit and well.
Letters sent, Love to all

On 8 May, Dennis's Battalion was deployed to the rapidly developing contest over the village of Potsangbam.

The regimental diary describes the battle that followed as one of the hardest fought actions in which the battalion was engaged.

The Battalion CO Col. McCready wrote the following account:[8]

> *It was estimated at this time that Potsangbam was held by approximately one company of Japanese. This estimate proved to be extremely inaccurate. The village itself was shaped something like a mushroom, with the stalk pointing north, the main part of the village being to the east of the road … it was the usual Manipuri village, with rather pleasant bamboo constructed huts, but with thick clumps of trees and bamboo. Visibility within the village was not more than 30 yards*

---

8 Bugle & Kukri: The story of The 10th Princess Mary's Own Gurkha Rifles (volume 1) By Colonel B.R. Mullaly.

and the bamboo clumps, particularly, made for-
midable obstacles for tanks. A fairly deep stream
ran through the village from east to west, and this
stream was definitely a tank obstacle. In short, the
village was ideally constructed for defence and we
knew our task would be no easy one.

Between 12-15 May, 1/10 GR were involved in operations
to capture the bridge at Potsangbam and to secure the village,
believing it to be held by an enemy in Company strength.

On 12 May, during an attack by C and D Companies,
C Company suffered thirty-five casualties from their own
artillery bombardment.

Dennis's Company was switched into the line at the
last moment, but the element of surprise was gone and
the attack faltered and was pushed back with a significant
number of British tanks lost in the process.

On 13 May, several crossings of the river were at-
tempted, but no new ground was held. Col McCready
noted later:

> *It was now quite obvious that we were going*
> *about this business the hard way and that, if we*
> *continued, we would suffer so many casualties in*
> *the 2 Bns that the final capture of Potsangbam*
> *would lose much of its attractiveness.[9]*

---

9   1/3 GR were also involved in the attack.

Battle of Potsangbam – Plan of the successful attack on the morning of 14 May 1944

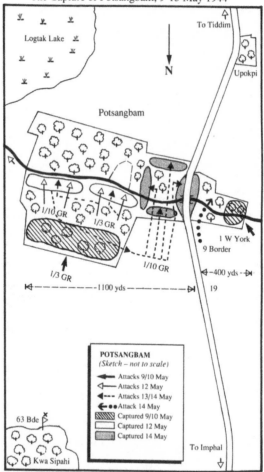

Map 11. The Second Battle of Bishenpur
The Capture of Potsangbam, 9-15 May 1944

Bugle & Kukri - The story of The 10th Princess Mary's Own Gurkha Rifles (vol 1) by Colonel B.R. Mullaly

At 1a.m. as a diversionary attack went in, A Coy and B Coy, led by Dennis, crawled across paddy fields in the dark and approached from the southern edge of the village launching a surprise attack which left the enemy "so bewildered that he put up a very poor fight."

The regimental diary reports:

> *Casualties were of course suffered, but mainly owing to Japanese booby-traps which had been laid along the edge of the village and which we could not see in the darkness. It was one such booby-trap that blew up Major Gwynne, resulting in the loss of an eye. Command of B Coy was taken over by Capt. Clarke and the operation proceeded smoothly.*

Potsangbam was finally rid of Japanese troops on 15 March and 1/10 GR was relieved and moved to Kwa Siphani to the north. The Battalion suffered five officer casualties and 200 from other ranks in the battle of Potsangbam.

The fighting from March to June 1944 on the Tiddim Road resulted in 6,740 British and Commonwealth soldiers being killed in action (around fifty per cent of all Allied deaths in the Battle for Imphal overall), in what was described as a fight to the death between the best fighting forces in the British and Japanese armies. The Japanese defeat at Imphal and Kohima was the largest suffered by the Imperial Army, with an estimated over 30,000 killed and 23,000 wounded. Over half of the Japanese soldiers who died did so from starvation or disease.

1 June 1944
Telegram from Leslie Gwynne

Dennis in hospital wounded in eyes, Left recovering right will take time. General condition good and cheerful and send his love. Address 47 B G H. Have seen him and written to you fully

---

On 6 June, D-Day was launched. The Allied invasion of Normandy, code named Operation Overlord, saw 160,000 troops cross the English Channel in the largest seaborne invasion in history.

14 June 1944
Airmail – from 47 BGH Calcutta;[10]

Received letters and have had them read to me by another of the patients who is also writing replies for me. I don't know what Leslie told you when he wrote but I will tell you what the doctors told me.

My general condition has very much improved, all the smaller wounds in my legs have healed up nicely, leaving no ill effects at all. My left eye is getting stronger all the time and I hope soon to able to begin reading and writing again. Will take every care and not risk straining it by overdoing things. I am afraid my right eye is not going to be any use but specialist told me that it will probably not be necessary to remove it. The small wounds on my face also healed and there will be no scars or disfigurement. Also, I have taken the opportunity of having a small operation on my big toes for ingrowing nails –would have been troublesome when I began marching again.

The treatment is good here and of course battle casualties are given priority. I have reached the stage when I can walk about in the ward and life is not quite so boring as it was when I had to lie in bed all the time with absolutely nothing to do. Being unable to read made

10 This begins, as all DHG's letters, with 'Dear Mum and Dad' but is not in his handwriting.

the time drag but now I sit around talking to the other patients and listening to the gramophone. Each morning I have newspapers read to me and we are all very interested to hear about the second front [**an interesting perspective on the Normandy landings! -Ed**].

I have met several Salopians in the hospital and have had a good gossip about our home county. It's always good to find someone who comes from Shropshire as it does not make us feel so far away. I was very glad to see Leslie when he walked into the ward one day and, during his stay in Calcutta, he visited me every day and brought me one or two things which I needed.

When I am discharged, I shall be given sick leave and will probably go to Bangalore and visit Norman.[11] After that I hope to be graded 'A1'again and be able to re-join my Battalion.[12] Please remember me to all who ask after me and tell them it was nothing really serious. I know how anxious you are about the three of us out here and how you worry, but please don't do so as I'm

---

11 Capital of the Indian state of Karnataka, South India.
12 In 1940, the British Army developed a system of seven medical categories; namely A1, A2, B1, B2, B3, B4, B5. Individuals were graded depending the degree of vision required for a list of specified military tasks. Once awarded, each grade then specified exactly what tasks could be carried out by that individual, whether at home or abroad. 'C' was fit for home service only. 'D' was temporarily unfit and 'E' was permanently unfit. Presumably, home service for a soldier serving in the Indian Army meant fit for service in India.

well and on the way to recovery. Received two copies of the *Wellington Journal* today and I shall look forward to reading them when I can.

20 June 1944
Airmail – 47 BGH Calcutta

You will be glad to hear that I am now practically recovered and that the vision of my left eye has been getting stronger all the time and is almost normal again. Lost the use of the right eye but it looks perfectly normal now that all the swelling etc. has gone down. It has been a great consolation all the time to know that my one eye was going to be OK and I think that has helped me to make a good recovery. Went out yesterday for the first time and had a walk around Calcutta and I felt much better for it when we got back. The bloke who does my letter writing came with me "just in case", but I'm glad to say I felt very confident I could look after myself. Things still appear rather blurred, but I'm told that as soon as I stop having drops put in the eye, everything will appear quite normal. I feel quite strong again and it is just a matter of time waiting for this eye to get OK.

Not yet begun reading or writing but I find it no strain to look at the pictures in the paper, although I cannot read the print. I have sometimes found it very boring just having to lie in bed but have been lucky in having a very cheery crowd of officers in this ward and that has helped a lot. I am arranging to meet Norman when I go on sick leave. He wrote saying he would endeavour to come here to see me, but I am being moved and shall be sent to Secunderabad which is much nearer his present station.[13] Hilda wrote saying she was rather worried as I had only been able to send a cable saying I had been wounded and was in hospital, am writing [**to her**] again shortly – drop her a line saying you have heard from me and that I am doing fine? I hope the next letter you receive will be written by me as I will be trying a bit of writing in a day or so.

The siege of Imphal is finally lifted on 22 June, when Milestone 107 on the Imphal/ Kohima road is captured and the road to Imphal re-opened.

---

13 The twin city of Hyderabad in the central Indian state of Telangana.

26 June 1944
Telegram from Leslie Gwynne

Letter written for Dennis says left eye greatly improved. Sight other lost. Tell Mum and Dad am progressing rapidly. Don't worry. Norman trying to visit Dennis

---

5 July 1944
Letter from Secunderabad (typed)

Dear Mum & Dad,

Much recovered and have been an "up" patient for some time so can walk about quite normally without hanging on to chairs and beds and anyone who happens to be passing!

My only trouble is my bad eye, the specialist has advised me to let him take it out and naturally I have agreed to have the operation. My left eye is quite safe at the moment and in time the vision will be perfect – but there is a danger that in time the other one which is "dead" will affect it and so he is removing this possibility. I can see quite well up to a distance of about 100 yards but it is not strong enough yet to take the strain of reading and writing. Keeping cheerful and occupied wandering around talking to other patients and listening to the wireless etc.[14]

A friend of Norman's called in and says Norman is trying to get short leave in order to visit me. I have written asking him to make it as soon as possible as after the operation I am being sent to Poona in order to have a glass eye fitted.[15]

When I am finally discharged from hospital it is doubtful that I will be allowed to re-join the Battalion and there is a possibility that I might be sent home. Please don't depend on this in any way as it is only a possibility. I understand that the specialist here will recommend it but whether it comes off or not is another matter. They won't need to ask me twice.

The hospital is very comfortable and we get first class treatment and food etc. Haven't contacted Barbara's friend, Sister Ryan, from St Dunstan's and I think she must be at some other hospital. Operation tomorrow.

---

14 Sometime after 5/7/1944, DHG's right eye was enunculated, although his medical records conflict on this point, in one case incorrectly stating the date as 29/6/1944. Enuculation is a procedure that involves cutting the optic nerve 'leaving the eye muscles and other orbital contents intact.'
15 Possibly the Deccan British Military Hospital in Poona or Pune, in the Indian State of Maharashtra, 100 miles SE of Bombay.

13 July 1944
Airmail from EM Cooper, 47th British General Hospital, India Command

Dear Mrs Gwynne,

I have received a letter from a friend, Olive Pearce, and she has asked me to write to you and give you detail of Dennis's condition. As far as I know, Dennis's brother saw the eye specialist when he was on leave and I expect he will have given you a fairly full account, but if there is anything I can tell you I shall be only too pleased. Dennis's main worry while he was with us was that you would be worried about him. The eye specialist here has every hope his left eye will have its full sight. His right eye will be of no further use but as the inflammatory condition is settling down well, he has not removed the eye but advised Dennis to have another opinion on his arrival in England.

When he left for Secunderabad three weeks ago his general health was very good and he was managing to get around quite well. His left eye is being kept at rest by having drops instilled. These drops make it impossible for him to see to read and write.

I had a letter from him written by another patient who went to Secunderabad with him and, on 29/6, the specialist told him that he would be on his way home very soon. Everyone who was on the ward with him was very sorry to see him go. He really is a very good patient and kept the ward cheerful. We were sorry he could not stay here longer, but no doubt you will be very pleased that he is, or soon will be, on his way home. I hope he will soon be home to fill in all the details.

18 July 1944
Telegram

Norman arrived.[16] *Staying three days. Am much improved. Have written letter. Love to all*

---

16 First meeting between Dennis and Norman since late 1941 or early 1942.

Lt Col A.N. Gwynne – HQ Southern Indian Army.

At last they meet. Dennis & Norman (centre) together on leave 1944

19 July 1944

Airmail, c/o Lloyds Bombay – [**letter written in his own hand, but much larger print than before, unsurprisingly -Ed**]

Many thanks for all your letter – it is nice to hear so many people had been asking after me and I felt proud to be a Gwynne. You must have been very busy dealing with all the enquiries. Would you send me the cuttings from the paper in which the information was published about me being wounded? I hope you gave them a good photograph!!! Also, I would like to know what the War Office said when they informed you about me. Do you think my writing has improved? My hand is still a bit unsteady and I find the pen shooting all over the place.

Sent cable so you would know Norman arrived ... at last. We had three days together and I was out with him most of the time. He introduced me to many of his old friends here so now I have plenty of visitors and I do quite a bit of visiting myself. He also arranged for me to have an Army car and a driver at my disposal whenever I wanted it!

Eye is getting on well and I'm taking great care of it. The specialist says there is no doubt the vision will eventually be quite normal and shouldn't take much longer now.

1 August 1944

Airmail – 1/10 GR c/o Lloyds, Bombay

The sight of my left eye has improved wonderfully since the right one was removed and is now practically perfect again. However, it is still rather weak in a bright light and waters a lot so I have to wear dark glasses when I go out. Reading and writing give me hardly any trouble now. Time passes much quicker now I have something to do. Before I used to get very fed up with nothing to do except lie in bed and I could barely see the people I was talking to – but that's all over now, and thanks to the wonderful treatment I've had you won't be able to see that anything has happened at all.

Waiting to go to Poona to get my glass eye put in and after that I get a Medical Board. Don't get thinking too much about what I said re: coming home – because as I have improved so well it probably won't come off.

Heard from Norman saying he had written home. Please thank all the kind people who enquire after me. Did Wellington get its £200,000?[17] The *Journal* is very welcome. I pass it on to the other Salopians here.

---

17 Possibly referring to war bonds appeal. In WW2 there was a Savings Campaign led by the War Office. In 1943, according to Hansard, the movement was raising £5m a week.

13 August 1944
Telegram

Discharged from Hospital. Spending leave with
Norman. Feeling fine. Love

---

1 September 1944
Airmail – 1/10 GR, c/o Lloyds, Bombay

Norman and I got back from Ooty on Monday and he is now back at work and I am staying until Sept 4th when I leave for Poona.[18] It has been very nice to be able to spend so long with Norman and I think he has enjoyed it as much as I have.

I had a Medical Board yesterday and have been graded 'C' for three months, after which I have another. I wasn't expecting a board until I got to Poona, but the authorities wrote and said I was to have it here. In a way it is a pity I could not have been sent home, but it means that my sight had improved so well that it is not now necessary. I feel fit and since leaving hospital have got quite brown again and put on a bit of weight. Will be passing through Bombay on my way to

---

18 A resort town in the Western Ghats mountains, Tamil Nadu, South India.

the Regimental Centre and can collect my mail then.

Hope all at home are well. I haven't heard from Barbara for some time. If you see Mrs Corbett ask her to remember me to Stanley. I expect he is in France now.

7 September 1944
Telegram

Leave over. Graded C. Posted Regimental Centre.
Norman well. Both send love

---

30 September 1944
Airmail, Alhilal Camp, Kangra Valley, Punjab

I am doing a training job and am in charge of about 900 recruits at the moment. It is quite interesting although I would rather be doing something a little more advanced – after all, I think I should know something about jungle warfare by now. I have another medical in three months and if I am OK will probably be graded 'B'. In any case, I think my active service days are over, for which I am sorry in a way. I realise how lucky I was in getting off so lightly. When I think of all the good friends I lost in Burma, I feel that perhaps I should carry on where I was before. Still, if I have to remain back here training more men, I shall have to stick it. I was very sorry to hear about Mr Drury I remember him very well.

Perhaps you would like to tell Colonel Oldham that I knew his son very well, Dad?[19]

We all thought him to be an extremely fine officer – a DSO and an MC don't come easily, you know. He was commanding a Battalion in the same Brigade as my old Battalion and the two were together in many actions in Burma.

I received the cutting from the *Express & Star* and am looking forward to seeing something in the *Journal* if it is in. I see they have put me down as aged twenty-three!! I'm twenty-six next August and will have six and a half years service. I will write to Betty soon and hope she and her son are doing well. I expect she would have preferred a daughter this time though.

I'm glad Lena is hearing from Norman now. I always tell him to write when I write to him and also said to him many times while we are on leave together. Today I received your number 130, Dad, telling me of Mrs

---

19 DHG was referring to Lt Col Wifrid Oldham, son of Col Frank Oldham, MC, DSO 4th Prince of Wales' Own Gurkha Rifles & Old Salopian, KIA 16 June 1944 in Burma and remembered by two windows and a tablet in St Peter's Church, Wrockwardine, Shropshire. Coincidentally, the same church Dennis was married in much later.

Vickers' legacy for me. That is very kind of her and will you please thank her for me? I have been told by the authorities my disability pension will be £135 per year and my present CO is getting out the necessary papers, enough to keep the wolf from the door anyway! Thank all those who ask after me, particularly Miss Jones and Mr Newman.[20]

6 October 1944

Receiving mail. Am fit and well, Congratulations to Betty and John, Love

12 October 1944
Airmail – c/o Lloyds Bombay

Two parcels of cigs arrived today (one of six tins and the other of four) for which many thanks. It's a long time since I had a good English smoke ... had been waiting for them forever since I first went into hospital and had almost given up hope. You said you had had one of the parcels that I sent and I hope you are finding the things useful. I asked the man to include some Kirby grips as I

20 Miss Jones was RG's secretary and Mr Newman was the Chief Clerk of R.Gwynne & Sons.

had heard that they were pretty scarce now. I am settled down here now and, as you know, my job is training new recruits.

The CO has arranged for me to have another medical board next month and with any luck I should be upgraded again but will still be remaining here, I think. Expecting the proofs of some photographs that I had taken on leave to come through soon and I will send some to you to act as proof that I still look the same!!

Wellington Journals continue to come along – I see that Vincent Greenhous' youngest son, Pat, has been killed – I was at school with him and knew him very well in the TA.[21] Also, I hear that Bill Alltree has been

---

21 Reports of the death of Pat Greenhous turned out to be somewhat premature. An ex-colleague of DHG's in 4 KSLI in 1939, Greenhous joined the RAF and was shot down on 14 May 1940 over Ostend in a Defiant (with 264 Sqn based at RAF Martlesham) after a dog fight in which his rear gunner shot down 2 ME109s. Pilot Officer Greenhous crash-landed but was captured and sent to Stalag Luft 3, Sagan in Poland.

In March 1944, Greenhous was one of 200 men who attempted to tunnel out of Stalag Luft 3 in what became known as 'the Great Escape'. Of the seventy-six prisoners who escaped, all but three were re-captured and fifty were executed on the orders of Adolf Hitler.

As news of the atrocities became public knowledge and confusion was rife as to the identities of those who had been killed, it would have been easy for DHG to assume his friend was dead. Pat Greenhous was freed in May 1945.

Coincidentally, the ME109s that shot down Pilot Officer Greenhous' Defiant just a few days after the invasion of France and the Low Countries, were from 5 Staffel, JG26, which from 6 June 1940 was commanded by Adolf Galland who eventually became General-in-command of Germany's fighter force and a highly decorated fighter ace with over 100 confirmed kills on the Western Front.

badly wounded, but I haven't heard from Stanley [Corbett] or Ted James for some time. It seems they have both got very "cushy" jobs – but don't say that to either of their mothers!! The news is very good, isn't it – we hear it every day on the overseas broadcast and hope that the war in Europe will be over this year and then we can really get going out here.

By October 1944, it was increasingly clear that the war in Europe would not be over that year.

There had been the initial success of D-Day in June. Over the summer, the Allies had made good progress across France and were poised to enter Belgium. Paris was also liberated in late August.

However, the failure of the audacious Allied airborne assault at Arnhem in September, in an attempt to capture a bridge across the Northern Rhine and bypass the German Siegfried defensive line, ended hopes of an early German surrender.

25 October 1944
Airmail – 10 GR Ahilal Camp, Kangra Valley

Three parcels of cigs arrived today, having been opened and packed up again. Luckily none of the tins had been pinched but the labels had been pulled off the outside wrapping, so I don't know whether they are the ones you sent. One parcel was on its way from Hilda so I have written thanking her for one of them and I'm now thanking you for the other. It's a long time since I had an English smoke and they taste very good. I'm glad to hear that one of my parcels has reached home safely – the first was posted in July, I think.

The *Journals* continue to arrive and make a pleasant change from the Indian newspapers we get. Not heard from Les or Norman recently and I hope Les enjoyed his leave. I'm feeling really fit – I don't think the doctors will find much wrong with me when I go up for my next medical board. The instructional work that I do is interesting and I have a pretty full day – I am on until 5.30 pm – I expect you and Reg can beat that though, Dad. Also, a lot of office work and I find that with the aid of my glasses, which I have for reading and writing, my eye gives me no trouble. It's really strong again now. Haven't heard from Barbara for some time – you would be glad to have her on leave when she manages it.

R Gwynne & Sons – Robert & Reginald Gwynne on the home front

12 November 1944

Dear Mum and Dad,

I am sending these photographs via a friend of mine who is coming home. On arrival I have asked him to post them to you. There are four of them and will you please send the fifth to Hilda? I think you know the address – 8 Wensley Road, Kensal, Manchester. Unfortunately, they won't arrive in time for Christmas but they will come quicker and safer like this than by the ordinary mail service.

It will be interesting to hear what you all think of them but, in any case, I think you would agree that I have not changed much and that my glass eye isn't very noticeable. In order to compare them I've also enclosed an old one of me taken in 1942 before I went to Burma. Also, one taken while in hospital and another while on leave. I heard from Leslie again saying he was back with his unit and had met Norman for a short while in Bombay. He was feeling much better for the rest and change and was ready to work again. I'm glad to hear Norman has been writing more frequently – I still don't know why he didn't do so before but he certainly was very busy.

27 November 1944

Airmail

Very fit and having no trouble with my eye, reading and writing is no strain and I'm now using my new glasses which are only very slightly tinted to take the glare off the sun. My left glass has a lens in it the right one is plain. Sunglasses are no longer needed. Taking every care and not straining it so don't worry.

Christmas is getting nearer and looking forward to my Christmas parcel. Two more lots of cigs came this week also several *Wellington Journals*. Glad to hear that Alan had been calling in while on leave, wish I could've been there to meet him – did he say where he was going next? Norman says John Jones was also home having been wounded in France. Frank Sharpe is home from Africa, I believe. My turn will come one day though then Wellington can really put the flags out!! Your Welcome Home Committee sounds interesting and I'm sure will be much appreciated.

Norman wrote yesterday off on some big exercise and thought he may get a better job if he did well on it. I wish Les could get some promotion, he certainly deserves it.

My medical board is due in about three days. I've been told unofficially that they will probably make me permanent category 'C' which means that I stay in this job or a similar one for the duration. What a life.[22]

5 December 1944
Airmail - Alhilal Camp, Kangra Valley, Punjab

Just finished writing to Alan in answer to a letter from him in Woolwich. He says it's grand to be back in the old Blighty again and I feel very jealous – however, I haven't so very long to do now before my time is up. The latest orders on repatriation say three years eight months so that gives me only another eleven months to go. All being well I should be with you next Christmas.

I was called before a medical board the day before yesterday but nothing very much happened as my papers from the last hospital were incomplete – however, they told me that when the time comes I shall be made a permanent category 'C' which is what I have been expecting. It will almost certainly keep me in this job until I come home. Leslie and Norman both written lately. Les had a move and is now on detachment and

---

22 Dennis was according to his medical records graded C Permanent on 20/7/1944, having been admitted on 15/7/1944 to hospital in Lahore with acute conjunctivitis in his left eye. His records also record that he was up-graded to B Permanent on 25/1/1945. See letter of 19 February 1945.

says he likes it better than previous place. Norman is still in Bangalore. No more now must get back to the office I'm now a chair-borne soldier!!!

19 December 1944
Telegram

Board C permanently. Very good wishes for Xmas and New Year, Love

---

1945

8 January 1945

---

*Parcel arrived safely. Had very good Christmas. Hope
all well at home. Am fit and well, Love*

---

14 February 1945

---

*Your cable recd. No news of such award here. Please
wire me source of information. Am fit and well. Hope
you both well, Love*

---

19 February 1945

Airmail – Achilal Camp, Kangra Valley, Punjab

Many thanks for your two cables about my MC. I must say I was a bit worried about the first one and I couldn't understand why you should hear before I did or my unit here did. I was also a bit scared that you had just heard a rumour, but I realise you wouldn't have sent me a cable unless you knew it to be true. I've had nothing official yet and so I cannot wear the ribbon or put MC by my name. I will cable you as soon as it comes through. I suppose being British Service attached to the Indian army, the citation would be sent direct to the War Office at home. I wish I was going to be at home when I get the actual medal presented, then you could come up to London and have a cup of tea with the King!! I don't know who will do it here but I will do my best to have someone nearby with a camera.

Today I received your most recent letter, Mum, dated 8 February in which you say Norman told you I had been to Karachi – actually it was Ranchi. [1] After that I went to Poona where I was re-examined – am now 'B' permanent and I think permanently here in the Regimental Centre. Glad to hear children fit. It must be hard going for you, have a good rest at Rhos and

---

1   Now the state capital of the Indian state of Jharkhand, W Bengal.

remember me to all there.[2] Your photos should be arriving any day now – the fellow I gave them to has reached Blighty, I think. Don't forget to send one to Hilda.

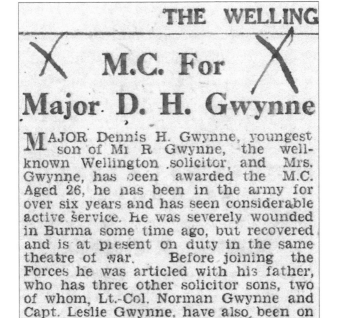

THE WELLING

M.C. For Major. D. H. Gwynne

MAJOR Dennis H. Gwynne, youngest son of Mr R Gwynne, the well-known Wellington solicitor, and Mrs. Gwynne, has been awarded the M.C. Aged 26, he has been in the army for over six years and has seen considerable active service. He was severely wounded in Burma some time ago, but recovered and is at present on duty in the same theatre of war. Before joining the Forces he was articled with his father, who has three other solicitor sons, two of whom, Lt.-Col. Norman Gwynne and Capt. Leslie Gwynne, have also been on active service for a considerable period.

It is interesting to note that some time ago Mr. R. Gwynne received a letter from the Shropshire Law Society, congratulating him on the fact that it was the first time in the society's history that four members of one family had been members of the society at the same time

Wellington Journal, **February 1945**

---

2   Maybe Rhos-on-Sea, Conwy, N Wales.

26 February 1945
Airmail – 10 GRC

Thank you very much for your letters of congratulations. I've had quite a few and I'm still feeling a bit dazed by it all. Actually, I was told some little time ago that I have been recommended for some award but didn't know which one and of course I didn't know whether or not the citation would be accepted. I think it rather than unlikely I shall ever see the actual citation so, if you want it, I think you had better get it from the War Office.

I would be glad if you would let me have a complete copy of the Military Supplement to the *London Gazette* because until I get that I have no authority for wearing the ribbon and it will probably take months for it to come through in the normal channels i.e. via the India Office to my unit here. I would also like the cuttings from the papers if possible. Norman wrote today saying that you have asked him for details, which he doesn't know and I really don't know myself and have a vague idea that it was the award given for a show I did last February but I'm not certain. At any date at any rate, the citation was apparently sent in long before I was wounded.

Glad to hear Dorrie staying for a few days with you – I'm sure you would've found her a great help and hope you're feeling the benefit.

5 March 1945

Letter from the War Office, London SW1 to R. Gwynne Esq, Edgbaston House, Wellington, Shropshire

Sir,

In reply to your letter of 13 February 1945, I am directed to inform you that the King has been graciously pleased to approve an award of the Military Cross to your son Capt. (T/Maj D.H. Gwynne (95010) K.S.L.I. (attd. 10 G.R.) in recognition of gallant and distinguished services in Burma and on the Eastern Frontier of India. An announcement to this effect was published in the *London Gazette* (No.36928) dated 8th of February 1945.

Copies of the *London Gazette* may be purchased direct from His Majesty's Stationery Offices or ordered through any bookseller (price 6d. Net)/

I have pleasure in enclosing for your information a copy of the statement which was submitted by the Commander-in-Chief, 11 Army Group, in support of his recommendation for this award. The unavoidable delay of this reply is regretted. I am, sir, Your obedient Servant,

Signed for

Lieutenant General, Military Secretary

Citation for the Military Cross

Captain (Temporary Major) Dennis Herbert Gwynne (95010) The King's Shropshire Light Infantry (attd. 10th Gurkha Rifles)

In the Chin Hills - 1944

On 27th of February 1944, Major Gwynne, commanding 'B' Company of a Battalion of the 10th Gurkha Rifles, was ordered to take his Company to the MUAL-BEM area, where operations were proceeding against the enemy.

He remained in this area until 10th March, 1944, and during this period, commanded his Company with great dash and initiative. As a result of his efforts 56 Japanese are known to have been killed and 13 wounded, with an unspecified number of possible casualties. His own company suffered two casualties, wounded. This result was achieved entirely owing to Major Gwynne's outstanding ability as a Company Commander.

During the withdrawal from TIDDIM, his Company was held in reserve in the first attack of 15th March 1944 by one Company of this unit, on the TUITUM Ridge Road-Block. His Company was skilfully disposed and gave valuable supporting fire to the attacking Company, being instrumental in breaking up an enemy attempt to collect and counter-attack the right rear of the forward Company.

On 16th March, 1944, in the Battalion attack on the same Road-Block, carried out by another unit, Major Gwynne's Company with great speed and following the artillery barrage so closely that 6 of his men were wounded, captured the feature then known as Left Knoll. His Company, his leadership was so quick on to the objective that any remaining enemy were unable to organise a successful defence and fled in confusion. The success of the operation was again due to Major Gwynne's speed and determination.

During the period 18th March to 26th March 1944, Major Gwynne's Company formed part of the forward defences covering the TUITUM Ridge area. The Company scored many notable successes during this period, inflicting many casualties, under his direction, on the enemy while making raids from his defended area.

On the night of 8th/9th April, 1944, Major Gwynne, with two Platoons of his Company was ordered to occupy a position on the MAPAO feature, which was reported clear of the enemy. Major Gwynne reached this position by night and found the enemy in occupation. At dawn, Major Gwynne attacked the position but was held up by fire from 2 medium machine-guns, 6 light machine-guns, a 4" mortar and Grenade Dischargers. Undeterred by this formidable defence, Major Gwynne regrouped his force and attacked again. He was driven back. For the third time he attacked the enemy position, but by then it had been reinforced and there was no hope of being able to drive the enemy out with the force at his disposal. Major Gwynne slightly withdrew his force and remained in a position of observation until ordered to return to his unit area.

The determination to get to grips with the enemy and the offensive spirit shown in the above actions are typical of Major Gwynne's conduct since he took over command of his Company.

He is an outstanding Company Commander and by his leadership has imbued in his men with the same fearlessness and determination which he, himself, shows on all possible occasions. In addition, he provides an inspiring example to all other officers.

7 March 1945
Airmail – **From Major D.H. Gwynne MC**

Received the copy of the *London Gazette* last week and an extract from that was published in our unit orders and my CO presented me with the ribbon which I am now wearing. I don't know when I will get the actual medal but, anyway, you can now stick MC after my name.

I don't know whether you noticed but in the same *Gazette* there were seven other MCs given to British and Gurkha officers of my Regiment. We haven't managed to get a VC in any of our Battalions yet although there is great competition going on as to which will get it first. Les and Norman both written to congratulate me and asked to know what I got it for but, as I haven't seen the actual citation, I don't really know myself.

There's a possibility at the moment that I may be called away from here to go to another job, but I hope not. Apparently, I am wanted for some staff appointment but my CO has replied saying that it is unwise for me to do a job with a lot of office work attached to it and on the strength of that I shall be left here. My eye feels no strain here and I only need to be in my office for a maximum of two hours a day. I'll keep you in touch but I think I shall be staying here.

REGIMENTAL CENTRE ORDERS
BY
COLONEL H. ST. J. CARRUTHERS, 10TH GURKHA RIFLES, COMMANDANT REGTL. CENTRE.
(ALMIL AL-K ANGRA VALLEY-PUNJAB) *****V***(SATURDAY THE 3RD MARCH 1945).
PART *** *** *** ** **1). No. 31.

1. HONOURS AND AWARDS.

Extract from the "London gazette" dated 6th Feb. 1945.

(i) The KING has been graciously pleased to give orders
for the following appointment to, the most excellent
Order of the British Empire, in recognition of gallant
and distinguished services in Burma and on the Eastern
Frontier of India:-

To be additional Officer of the Military Division
of the Said most excellent order:-
****

1A 147 Maj.(T/Lt.Col.) FRANCIS ROY SEPPINGS COSENS, D.S.O.

18731D Lieut.(T/Capt.) LEONARD CONRAD NICHOLLS
10TH GURKHA RIFLES.
————o————

(ii) The KING has been graciously pleased to approve the
following awards in recognition of gallant and distinguished
services in Italy:-

THE MILITARY CROSS.

10 15347 Jemadar Bekhendhoj Rai
10 13354 Jemadar Harkajit Rai
No. 5112 Rfn.(A/Nk) Sarke Rai
No. 5713 Lance Naik Dhansing Rai
10TH GURKHA RIFLES.
————o————

(iii). The KING has been graciously pleased to approve the
following awards in recognition of gallant and distinguished
services in BURMA and on the Eastern Frontier of India:-

THE MILITARY CROSS.

19601D Capt.(T/Maj.) Dennis Herbert Gwynne
1A 1547 Capt.(T/Maj.) Charles Michael Anthony Rookherst
Roberts.
4814 Subedar (A/...m.) Purna Rai, O.B.I.
864 Jemadar (A/Sub.) Karshchoj Rai
10TH GURKHA RIFLES.
————o————

THE MILITARY MEDAL.

No. 105110 Naik Kewaram Rai
—No. 105260 Rfn.(A/Nk) Gangabah ...r Rai
No. 2010 Lance Naik Amberbahadur Rai
—No. 2202 Lance Naik Chhabirsing Rai
No. 105298 Lance Naik Narbahadur Sunwar
No. 105681 Lance Naik Ramoo Rai
—No. 107519 Riflemen Panchadhoj Rai
10TH GURKHA RIFLES.
————oOo————

P. Barkley

Major,
10th Gurkha Rifles,
For Adjutant, Regimental Centre.
(R.J BARKLEY-EC6512).

L. B. DEWAN/-

Extract of the *London Gazette*

9 March 1945
Airmail

Received two letters from you today of 27th and 28th Feb. Sorry to hear that you had to go and see a specialist, Mum, and I hope he gave you a good report. Let me know when you write.

I'm looking forward to seeing the Law Society Scheme for Articled Clerks and I am anxious to know what they will do with us. It will be six years in August since I left the office – a lot of time to make up, isn't it? I have met many fellows out here who are in a similar position and they will be glad to know as well. I'm afraid I missed writing to Betty for Robert's birthday, wish him many happy returns for me.

Talking about the MC being the fourth after the VC, its third actually and ranks equal with the DSC (Navy) and the DFC (RAF), The only trouble is it doesn't carry any pension with it, I don't think!!

Les wrote, he mentioned the possibility of home leave but, being Indian Army, would only be leave. Norman and I are British Service attached and become due for repatriation after three years eight months, but whether or not we get it is another thing. It's just begun raining – the first rain since the last monsoon, so I hope it doesn't come too early this year.

12 March 1945
Airmail

I have today received your letter of 3rd March saying you have had a letter from Gerry Gardner and also the photos. I think you are right when you say I look fuller in the face as I certainly have put on quite a lot of weight since leaving hospital. About the photos being touched up a bit – I don't think they did that at all and you will find, I hope, that my glass eye matches the other one very well.

Your telegram came today as well saying the citation was in the post, I'm looking forward to reading it. You will know by now that on receipt of that copy of the *London Gazette* everything became official out here and I am now wearing the MC ribbon. I was very glad to read that Mother is much better – the warmer weather will make all the difference, Mum, and I hope you will continue to improve.

You will see that the date of this letter is 12345 i.e. 12/3/45 and I'm told that only happens once every hundred years, so I suppose it's a day to be remembered. No fresh news about anything here.

21 March 1945

Airmail

Just been writing to Auntie Ida and Barbara in reply to the letters. You will be on your holiday now and I hope you're feeling the benefit. We aren't having any special holiday here owing to the pressure of work but I shall make up for it when I get my leave. I shall be entitled to twenty-eight days this year as opposed to fourteen last year and I think I will either go up to Kashmir or Darjeeling, neither of which places I have seen yet.

I heard from Major Gerry Gardner this week saying you had written to him. Willie Houle also wrote. I'm glad you met him – he is hoping to come back here as a civilian shortly and get a Civil Service job in Burma. Personally, when I get to England, wild horses won't get me away again!!

24 March 1945

Airmail

Received two parcels of cigs – ten tins in all. Also, your mail letters of 13/3 enclosing two cuttings and your other airmail with the citation. I handed this over together with a copy of the *London Gazette* to my CO here and it has been put with my service records. As you know by now, everything is official and you can write MC behind my name. About the actual presentation in the medal itself as opposed to the ribbon, I don't know when that will be done.

Your AM letters come very quickly, only about two to three days slower than AMLCs and, of course, much cheaper. Thank Connie [RG's housekeeper] for her message, also Mrs. Cotton (wool)!! Tell Connie I haven't tasted a macaroni pudding since I left home so she had better be ready to make one the great day when I arrive. I'm also glad to hear you are much better, Mum. Connie will be a great help for you. Take things easy now.

I wrote to Norman yesterday. Ootacamund [Ooty] is a very nice hill station about 130 miles SW of Bangalore in the Nilgri hills. Glad you like the photo – Hilda says she does. Heard that Maj Willie Hoole has now been discharged from the Army.

16 April 1945

Fit and well. Am receiving mail. Sent another parcel.
Love to all.

16 April 1945
Airmail

I am well although very busy. I sent you a wire yesterday as I haven't been able to write for a week or so. Have you received any money lately? I told the bank to send off Rs.1000 which should come to about £70 odd. When you have time would you please let me know how much I have in War Savings and my PO a/c. I think the money is better at home I don't want to keep too much in my a/c here.

I have had a letter from the Law Society telling me about Articled Clerks etc. and was interested to hear what they are going to do for us. I shall feel quite an old man going back to the University when I'm twenty-seven or thereabouts – that is, providing I can get out of the army by then. I've just been reading the Gough manslaughter case in the paper. Have we had a hand in it at all? I see Gough-Thomas was originally defending.

Another parcel of tea is on the way for April – next one will be in May. Did you go to Rhos?

Operation Dracula was launched on 1 May 1945 at the mouth of the Rangoon river. The amphibious assault by a division of 15 Corps along with a Gurkha Parachute Battalion, secured the coastal batteries and cleared the river of mines. The force entered Rangoon the following day, without opposition, effectively concluding the liberation of Burma.

7 May 1945
Airmail

I've just written to Delhi and asked the food parcel company to send off your monthly parcel. I have now sent one for February, March, April and May – hope they are getting through. My cigs are coming along well and last week I had four tins from Auntie Ida so I have sent her food parcel this month. I was pleasantly surprised to see how much my savings had accumulated to. Now that I can't get any more War Savings please put it all into the PO.

I shall be needing a lot of it for new clothes etc. when I get home. On release from the army we get a grant to £12-12s for mufti.[3] I've no more news about repatriation, I'm merely hoping I get it when it becomes due in October. It doesn't seem over three years since I left home does it? I'm told I don't get any priority for release for being a student or medical category B so I

---

3   Mufti was a British Army term for civilian attire, probably dating from the early nineteenth century and referring to the habit of wearing eastern style gowns and caps by off-duty officers in the style of a Mufti, or Islamic scholar.

have to wait for my normal release number to come up. Mine is 26 and I don't suppose I should be out before the end of Japan.

We are all eagerly awaiting the end of Germany here as we are getting two days holiday. They say only Czechoslovakia is left now so it can't be long.

Many thanks for the *Law Society Gazette*. Like me, I expect you would have preferred to see my name in it as having been admitted. I wonder how long that will take.

Hitler commits suicide in Berlin on 7 May 1945. Two days later, on 9 May 1945, Soviet troops enter Prague.

15 May 1945
Airmail

Well our short holiday is over and we are all back at work now, working for VJ day which is what we are all really interested in. By the time it comes I hope the three of us will be home to celebrate it with you. I've no more news about my repatriation except for I'm due in November and I'm hoping they won't keep me long after that. Norman and Leslie also due about then and it would be grand if we could all be on the same boat.

What's all this Barbara has been telling you about Hilda and I? Les mentioned in his last letter. What I did tell Barbara was that it may happen but only after I got myself settled after the war.

The news in Burma is very good, isn't it? I wish I could be with them now that we've got the Japs on the run. I would like to have seen Rangoon. There's not much news from here, I'm still doing the same job.

It's getting very hot again now and the rains will be here shortly. I managed to listen to the England v Wales soccer the other day on the wireless, did you hear it? We also heard Mr. Churchill's first announcement but not his speech or the King's.

Wales v England football friendly was played at Ninian Park, Cardiff, on 5 May 1942 in front of 25,000 people. England won 3-2.

At 3pm on Tuesday 8 May 1945, Winston Churchill addressed the nation and later made an impromptu speech from the Ministry of Health known as the "This is your victory" speech. The former is possibly the announcement DHG heard, the latter the speech he missed.

The King also addressed the nation from Buckingham Palace on 8 May 1945 and reminded the country that "in the Far East we have yet to deal with the Japanese, a determined and cruel foe."

21 May 1945
Airmail

Your letter dated 12th instant arrived today telling me that you have had two days VE holiday. We had a good time too but what we really want is VJ day.

It's a long way from over yet and you mustn't hope too much that the end of Germany will speed up my return as much as all that, and I don't see any chance of coming before my time is up which isn't much longer really. Also, I don't think the release of my group 26 will be announced before the end of Japan. I hope it will be but I don't think so. Les and Norman both hope to be on their way at the end of the year and, with luck, should all three be with you for Christmas or early in the New Year.

I'm so glad to hear you are managing to get away to Rhos after all and hope you will have a good time. Have the food parcels arrived yet? My cigs and journals continue to roll in – they are very welcome.

29 May 1945
Airmail

You will be back from Rhos by now and I hope you're feeling the benefit of your short holiday. Major Gardner has arrived back in India but he has not reached here yet.

I have some very good news for you today. I have recently been appointed second in command of the whole depot here, and with luck it will mean a promotion and, of course, an increase in pay. I do not expect to hold the job for long as I know that a regular officer has been asked to fill the vacancy. I am merely like Mr. Churchill, a temporary caretaker. So, don't be worried if I say that I have been made a Lt-Colonel and then a week later I tell you that I'm down to Major again. Naturally, I shall do all I can to hold onto the job but, as I say, an older and regular commissioned officer has been asked for. The regular army doesn't like to think these youngsters can do one of the bigger jobs. However, we shall see.

Lt Colonel DH Gwynne, MC – 2 i/c of 10GR Regimental Training Centre, Alkilal Camp, Kangra Valley in 1945

Close up with eye patch

7 June 1945

Airmail

It's 10 pm and I'm sitting in my room getting a few letters off. It's very hot here lately and I'm wearing just a pair of pyjama trousers and I still feel hot. The nights are worse than the days, I think, although it's pretty bad in the office with the temperature well over 100°F. The new job is going very well and my eye is not noticing any strain due to the extra paperwork.

No promotion yet but it may not be long now. That is provided the new bloke doesn't arrive too soon. The rules for our leave on repatriation are just out and we get 56 days and, in addition, one day extra for every month abroad so that will make about three months, and all on full pay too! I think my repat will almost certainly come before my demobilization so with any luck I may only have to serve a short while again after my leave and then get demobbed. Norman says his demob number is 17 so he will be out quite a bit before me.

Gerry Gardner arrived this evening but he has not yet unpacked his trunk and I haven't seen my parcel. However, it has come quite safely. He looks very fit and says England is just wonderful. I don't think he likes coming away again much – though his peacetime job is out here anyway. He wishes me to thank you again for the cigs you sent him.

On 15 June 1945, King George VI dissolved Parliament for the first General Election since 1935 and the election was called for 5 July 1945.

The wartime coalition led by Sir Winston Churchill had come to an end on 23 May 1945, with Churchill continuing as PM at the head of a caretaker government. (Note: DHG's reference to Mr Churchill in letter of 29/5/45).

20 June 1945
Telegram

Promoted Lieutenant Colonel, Receiving Mail,
Fit and well, Love

---

20 June 1945
Airmail

I'm writing this with the new pen that you sent me – it seems to suit my hand very well. Thank you again for the parcel, everything was OK and I'm still enjoying the cigs. The snaps are all very good though I must confess that I had some difficulty in recognising some of my nephews and nieces!! Don't tell their mothers. You both look fit and well and have not changed at all. Barbara too looks very fit.

You had my cable by now telling you that I have been promoted. While it lasts the increase in pay is going to be very welcome. My net will now be about 1715 rupees a month and in pounds and shillings that sounds very nice.

The new job is going well. I spend most the day at my desk and usually finish about 6.30 pm. The afternoons are so hot that it is practically impossible to work inside so I stay outside after lunch until about 4.30 pm, when it begins to cool off a bit. The monsoon is due to start on the 25th so that will make it a bit better.

No more news about my repat, but at least I am certain of being home for Christmas – I hope. If Leslie gets his transfer, he will be eligible for repat – at the moment, as he is in the Indian army not just attached like Norman and I, he is not.

23 June 1945
Airmail

Well I'm still holding down the new job and everything seems to be going very well. If I can hang on to the extra pip for another two months that will make me a permanent Major, otherwise, I will be in danger of dropping to Capt again on the return home. No rank is permanent until you have held the next highest for a total of three months. It's a funny system but that's the army. I expect Babs will be able to explain it to you or perhaps they work it differently in the RAF?

I'm expecting shortly to have my MC presented officially, but I can't say much now. I will tell you about it when it's all over, will have a snap or two taken for you.

Have you heard anything of either Stan Corbett or Alan Benson lately? Wrote to them both a little while ago, no reply. You might mention it to Mrs. C and Mrs. B if you meet them in town at all. Weather is getting really sticky although it won't be as hot as down in the plains – it's almost unbearable down there in the hot weather.

On 5 July 1945, the British General Election took place with counting delayed to 26 July in order for overseas votes by service personnel to be brought home and counted.

First Tour by a commander-in-chief in India of military units in the Kangra Valley for 20 years has just been made by Gen. Sir Claude Auchinleck. Among the regimental centres he visited was that of the 10th Gurkha Rifles at Alhilal. Here he is seen presenting the MC (won in Burma) to Lieut. Col. D.H. Gwynne, of Eversleigh, Wellington, Shropshire.

Picture courtesy of InterServices Public Relations Directorate, India C-in-C visits Gurkha Units in Kangra Valley

14 July 1945
Airmail

Many thanks for your letter of 4th enclosing more snaps. The children are growing up, aren't they? Glad to hear the parcels are coming through, it's a pity about the sugar. The parcels are already made up when they we buy them and I always get the ones with the most tea and it usually has sugar in as well. I will keep on sending as often as possible.[4]

About the election, I filled in a proxy form some time ago, but apparently you haven't had it? It's too late now so there's nothing else I can do.

I hope you are back home from Quarry Place now and feeling much better. Your news about having to have the injections worried me a bit but they will do you good, I expect. Let me know how you are. No further news to report, will let you know as soon as anything happens. I think you will be seeing me before Christmas.

---

4 Tea and sugar, along with all foodstuffs with the exception of bread and vegetables, were rationed in Britain from 1940. Loose Tea was being rationed at 8oz per adult per week and sugar at 2oz per week in 1945 and remained subject to rationing until October 1952 in the case of Tea and late 1953 in the case of sugar respectively. Furthermore, anyone receiving parcels from abroad of over 5lbs was liable to have this deducted from their food ration. The continuation of rationing and austerity measures were major issues in the 1950 General Election, which saw Labour's majority cut to just five seats.

19 July 1945
Airmail

The monsoon has really started here and the heat is terrific. The rain doesn't seem to lower the temperature at all and I think it is even worse during the night than during the day.

I hope you're feeling much better by now, Mum, and that your stay in Quarry Place has done you good. What you need is a long holiday at the sea or some nice weather. Perhaps we will be able to have it next year, all together again.

Graham [Murphy] wrote to me last week and said that if all goes well, I might get away about October. It is by no means official, of course, but he is supposed to know something about these things. I hope he's right! Norman is due before me so I might be able to gauge my repat from the date that he goes. Haven't heard from Leslie for a few weeks, don't know whether he has had any luck over his transfer to British Service. Is Barbara still at home? When is she getting released?

Labour Leader Clement Attlee became Prime Minister on 25 July 1945 as Labour won the election by a landslide majority of 148 seats with an overall swing of 12% (both the size of the majority and the swing remain post-war records).

25 July 1945

Airmail

Very glad to know you are feeling much better, Mum. It is a nuisance having to have injections twice a day, but it is well worth it if they are really doing you good.

The weather should help you as well now, or isn't it as nice as it should be? It's so hot and sticky here I have to change at midday because I get absolutely soaking with perspiration working indoors and outside, of course, you get soaked with rain.

I note in your letter that Norman says I should come out of the army as I left – Lt Col. I wonder where he gets that from? Until Aug 24th my permanent rank is Captain. If I'm still a Lt Col after that date, my permanent rank goes up to Major and therefore at the best I get out as a Major. However, all I want to be is a plain Mister again!! I can manage OK for cigs and I don't really think it's worth sending any more – I may get a call any time next month and I should miss them.

The Allies called for the unconditional surrender of Japan under the Potsdam Declaration of 26 July 1944, which Japan ignored.

Faced with the prospect of a costly invasion of mainland Japan and the increasing involvement of the Soviet

Union in the theatre, who formally declared war on Japan on 9 August 1945, the Allies decided to use atomic weapons, the first and, to date, only use of such weapons in armed conflict.

On 6 August 1945, the US dropped an atomic bomb on Hiroshima and three days later on 9 August 1945, a second atomic bomb on Nagasaki. In excess of 200,000 people (mainly civilians) were estimated to have been killed as a direct result of the two blasts.

9 August 1945
Airmail

My birthday went off very quietly. I was very busy on that particular day and didn't have much time to think about it. Thank you for the cable, which arrived on the morning of the second, and also your letter. Babs wrote to me. She said you looked much better when she left home. It would be nice having her for a bit – it's a pity she can't get released and be with you all the time.

I've heard no more about my coming home, but I think October will be about it. You won't be able to meet me before I get to Wellington as nobody is allowed to meet the boats and, in any case, I shan't know which port I shall be landing at. All I will be able to say is when I am leaving India and then wire or phone when I land. Anyway, I will give you all the news when the time gets nearer. Have been very busy, the CO is away and I'm in charge for the moment.

On 15 August 1945, VJ Day, Emperor Hirohito announced the surrender of Imperial Japan. The formal instrument of surrender was signed aboard the USS Missouri in Tokyo Bay on 2 September.

Prime Minister Atlee thanked Britain's allies in Australia, New Zealand, India, Burma and all countries occupied by Japan, but especially the US "without whose prodigious efforts the war in the East would still have many years to run."

On 16 August 1945, King George VI addressed the nation from Buckingham Palace. "Our hearts are full to overflowing, as are your own. Yet there is not one of us who has experienced this terrible war who does not realise that we shall feel its inevitable consequences long after we have forgotten our rejoicings today."

Interestingly, Dennis makes no mention of the Hiroshima bomb in his letter of 9 August. Furthermore, there are no surviving letters, telegrams or correspondence of any kind from Dennis for the period from 9 August to 2 September 1945, a period that included the dropping of the second atomic bomb on Nagasaki, the formal Japanese surrender and VJ Day itself.

It is hard to believe that for such a regular correspondent, and given how much he had yearned for this outcome as well as the cost to him personally in terms of injury and the death of friends and men under his command, that he would let this final victory pass without any comment at all. But it is also entirely understandable if he just chose to keep his thoughts and emotions to himself, unable or unwilling to process the magnitude of the actions and events he had witnessed. Another explanation might be that he simply could not write about any of this to his parents at all – and therefore there are no letters that survive in the 'Dear Mum & Dad' collection I have in my possession. Perhaps he wrote instead to Hilda, or to his two brothers in India who could at least understand what he had experienced and what the end of the Japanese war meant to those who had fought in it.

Aside from the surrender leaflet which Dennis kept with his papers, there are no references at all in any of his subsequent correspondence for the rest of his time in India to the war or the victory over Japan either. A possible reason for this may be something that was alluded to in Dennis's obituary in the Bugle & Kukri in May 1973, which mentioned his invaluable service at Ahilal 'not least during those last difficult days on the British Raj'.

Given how rapidly the situation was developing from

mid-1945, maybe Dennis was by then more pre-occupied with the increasingly difficult position of the British in India and getting home as soon as possible than he was about the recent defeat of Japan.

The change of Government in Britain in 1945 and the role of the Indian Army played in the defeat of Japan, as well as calls from Gandhi and Nehru for British troops to leave India from mid- 1945, set in chain a seemingly unstoppable series of events that would lead to Indian Independence in 1947.

Japanese leaflet dated 18 Aug 1945 describing Japan's unconditional surrender – possibly for distribution by the Allies to Japanese units in Burma.

Although Nepal, as an independent country, was not impacted directly by Indian Independence, uncertainty over the future of the Gurkha Regiments post-Independence was only eventually resolved in 1947.

2 September 1945
Airmail

I have just been warned to standby for a move at the end of this month so I should be seeing you sometime towards the end of October with any luck. I'll keep you posted and, if possible, will let you know when I actually leave. Les wrote saying his transfer was through and he is on his way by now, I expect. I haven't heard from Norman for some weeks, I feel sure he must've left. Both he and Les are overdue for going home now. I'm very excited about my repat and I can hardly think of anything else. Christmas should see us all around the table again.

I returned from a few days leave two days ago and have been very busy catching up with work and feel much better for the rest and change and managed to buy a few clothes which I shall be needing at home. Shopping is pretty difficult here but at least there is much more in the shops than at home.

As I have been expecting sooner or later, I am again

down to Major. An officer senior to me has arrived and, although he has not taken my job, he had got my rank. Still, I held it for more than the requisite three months and am now a permanent Major and won't go lower on return home.

Anyway, it won't be long before I have the best rank of all – just plain Mr! That will be about January, I hope. I had a very unexpected letter from Derek this week and have replied. He is quite ok – tell Uncle Will he seems to be enjoying the life.

9 September 1945
Airmail

Time is drawing close now and I am beginning to get that end of term feeling. I've been going through my kit and seeing what can be left behind as I can only bring for 4 cwt in all. During the last six months, living more or less under peacetime conditions, I seem to have collected quite a lot of stuff which will have to be left behind. However, 4 cwt is quite a lot and I should not be losing anything much.

No definite dates have been given to me yet but I hope to sail very early in October. Both Leslie and Norman will have gone by then they may even be on their way now, so you'll be seeing them before me. Won't know where I am landing, will phone or wire you as soon as I can so you will know when to expect me in Wellington. It's going to be a great day isn't it? I sent you another Rs.1000 (£75 pounds approx.) this week to Lloyd's.

When I leave, I will ask Lloyds, Bombay to transfer my entire account to you and then I can open my own a/c again when I have discussed things with you. Can take a little for the journey in travellers' cheques.

30 September 1945
Airmail

Nothing through about my move yet but I'm expecting it daily – whenever the official mail comes in I dash along to the office and watch it being opened but so far, I've had no luck. It must come within the next day or so. All my bags are already packed and I can be away as soon as I get the word. Graham Murphy wrote a few weeks ago saying he was hoping to travel with Norman, which will be nice for them. With luck I should meet some of the fellows I came out with when I get to the transit camp.

From now on I would stop writing, I think, as I shan't get them much longer. I'll leave a forwarding address of course, but they will have to go back home again before I see them, so please hold any letters that you received from me from now on.

15 October 1945

Leaving Alhilal sixteenth. Hope to be with you by early November. Am well, Love

---

21 October 1945
Airmail – from Homewood Bound Trooping Depot

I've now arrived this far and am waiting for our party to be detailed for a boat. One of the first people I met was Les, who got here two days ago. He will probably be sailing about the 23rd-24th and I shouldn't be far behind him. I told him that you had heard from Norman and that by now you must've seen him home at last.

I had two days in Bombay before I came here and, on the evening of the 19th, I watched one boat sail out which is due home on Nov 13th. Most of them are taking even less time than that now about 16-20 days – pretty good to what it took us coming out here.

There's very little to do except for wait so I'll try to write another again before I leave. Right now, I have a lot of forms to fill in so I'll finish. In haste with love to both.

At the end of the war, there were approximately 5 million servicemen and women in the British Armed Forces.

Demobilisation was a huge logistical challenge and was prioritised in essence on an age-and-service number basis, with some priority given to married women, men over fifty and personnel with university places, hence the different release categories.

By the end of 1945, 750,000 service personnel had been de-mobbed and this number doubled in the months post VJ Day.

There was a lot of frustration over the slow pace of demobilisation, leading to disciplinary issues such as the RAF mutiny of 1946 in India.

It wasn't only returning personnel who found re-assimilation difficult, however. The 1947 divorce rate wouldn't be exceeded until the 1960s.

29 October 1945

Expect me not later twentieth. Leslie already sailed.
Met him here. Both well, Love

On 29 October 1945, Dennis's Battalion, 1/10 Gurkha Rifles, took the formal surrender of the Japanese 28th Army in Burma.

4 November 1945

Airmail - SS Winchester Castle, Port Said

I'm writing this as we steam up the Red Sea. It will be posted at Port Said, where we stop for a few hours. We passed Aden yesterday and are due at Port Said sometime on Tuesday. So far it has been a very calm voyage and of course very hot, but when we get into the Med it should cool down and we shall want some warm clothes again. If all goes well, we should dock in England – either Southampton or Liverpool – on the 15th or 16th and as I said before I will phone you as soon as possible.

There are about 3,000 troops on board and I think we are all finding it a bit difficult to realise that we are at last going home.

Apparently, some sort of civic reception has been arranged for us, but I don't quite know what it is. The main thing is to let us get to our homes with as little fuss as possible. By the way when you see me, I shall be wearing a black patch over my eye. Don't worry I've got to get a new glass eye in England.

The *SS Winchester Castle* – built in 1930 by Harland & Wolff, Belfast. The *SS Winchester Castle*, participated during WW2 in no less than 3 invasions including N Africa, Sicily and Operation Dragoon, the invasion of S France in August 1944. Interestingly, her official capacity was listed at 189 first class passengers and 398 tourist class – so 3,000 must have been a squeeze!

Although this collection of letters ends at this point, Dennis remained in the Army as a Territorial officer with the rank of permanent Major until he was demobbed on 3 August 1946, and was granted 100 days leave from 25 April.

My father Michael (MTG) has always maintained that that for a time after returning from India and before his discharge, Dennis was the commandant of a POW camp, possibly in Herefordshire.

The only POW camp listed in Herefordshire was Camp 27 at Ledbury, which held around 700 Italian and Ger-

man prisoners from 1941 onwards. The commandant commanding the camp in 1945 was a Major Gillingham (who was actually only appointed in 1945), so Dennis's rank would have been appropriate and he could, in theory, have been appointed in early 1946.

MTG also remembers Dennis telling him that a high-ranking Nazi had 'escaped' whilst under his command (possibly a General whose name started with 'Mann').

The only recorded break out by German POWs was in March 1945 from Camp 198, near Bridgend in South Wales, so those dates wouldn't work. Interestingly, from 1946 this camp was re-designated Special Camp 11 under the command of a Major Topham, for high-ranking Nazi's awaiting war crimes trials.

Notable German POWs held here included a certain Field Marshall Eric Von Manstein (captured in August 1945 and who gave evidence at Nuremburg in 1946).

Family myth or fact? Who knows, but Ledbury and Bridgend aren't so very far apart...

Did Wolverhampton Forget
The Yeomanry?

GOSSIP

VIGILANT

STAFFORDSHIRE YEO-MANRY — On Saturday last I visited Burton-on-Trent to witness the conferring of the freedom of the borough on the North Staffordshire Regiment and the Staffordshire Yeomanry. I have previously visited Stafford and Lichfield, where this honour was also given to the yeomanry and other regiments. These three towns have all shown publicly their appreciation of all that the yeomanry have done during the war, whilst Wolverhampton fairs once more to acknowledge their fine record, even though the 4 press and that once informed us that the Staffordshire Yeomanry are first everywhere. This is true of everywhere, except Wolverhampton. —ONLOOKER.

DAVID TEARLE, who has all the Tearle family couples enormous physique with a fine profile, is almost at home ground in appearing at Dudley Hippodrome this week. When I talked to him in his dressing-room at the interval of "Lorna Doone" in which he is playing the part of handsome-born John Ridd, he told me that he had spent some of his boyhood at Summer Hill.

David Tearle

area well," he said, "and I have great affection for the Midlands was born in Monday."

David, who is a cousin of Godfrey Tearle, spent two years touring America in stage shows prior to the war and found time to play a part in George Arliss's film "Queen Goddess."

Judging by his performance last night he is obviously in the front rank of British actors and it was encouraging to hear him say that he would not be returning to America.

I should like to see him in films for he has the boldness and dash to equip him for those Technicolor historicals which have been so sadly missed since the good old days of Douglas Fairbanks.

His Ambition

A 13-year-old Dudley boy has written his own Christmas pantomime, is playing the principal part, and is also producing it. His name is Leo Benson, the only son of Mr Jack Benson, stage manager at the Dudley Hippodrome who lives at 99 Priory-road Dudley. Leo, who is a solicitor at the Intermediate School, has given several shows to aid of men of the Merchant Navy during the war. The pantomime, for which Billy Hands, conductor of the Dudley Hippodrome Orchestral has written special music, will run for a whole week in aid of St Christopher's Church.

Leo Benson

His father told me last night that since an early age Leo had wanted to go on the stage. He wants to be a conjurer, and is already quite expert in the art. "I shall do all I can to encourage his stage ambitions," said Mr Benson.

Plate for Little Miss Muffett in the pantomime will be five-year-old Derby.

SEDGLEY HOUSING — The statement I was endeavouring to draw from certain councillors was why a recent vacant council house was allocated to a newcomer to the district. — N. A. JONES, Upton-road, Sedgley.

ARMY RELEASE. — I agree entirely with R.A.F. India, with regard to the disparity in the general release between the three services. For instance, Army group 48 is supposed to be out by the end of this year, which means that these fellows will have served three and a half to four years, perhaps longer. Group 59 in the navy is also due for demobilisation by the end of the year, with probably two years service in. Why should there be this vast difference? Perhaps our local MP's will look into this matter; but that we and the navy groups got back, but let's have the army and R.A.F. sported up to bring them on more equal terms. — EX-SERVICEMAN, 1914-18.

No Tyres

THE Rev J. K. Thomson, of the Union Free Church, Constitution-hill, Wellington, has just returned from a fortnight's stay in Holland, where he and his wife were in charge of a party of 25 children from the Wrekin area.

With headquarters at Bossum, the Shropshire children, one of six different parties of English and girls, toured Holland by train (tramcar, canal and on foot) visiting a large number of centres of historical and industrial interest.

A noticeable feature, Mr Thomson tells me, was the tremendous number of cycles in use and the almost complete absence of tyres. Lacking covers for their cycles, the Dutch career about on the rims of their cycles apparently oblivious to the deafening noise.

The visit is part of a scheme of the World Friendship Association to make holidays possible for a possibility for thousands of ordinary adults as well as children. In the near future, and on Saturday next Dutch children begin a visit to Wellington and district.

M.C. By Post

AFTER waiting two years Lieutenant - Colonel Dennis Herbert Gwynne (27) youngest son of Mr and Mrs Robert Gwynne, of Eversleigh, Millbank, Wellington, has yesterday awarded the Military Cross—by post!

Colonel Gwynne won the award in Burma in 1944, where, in later fighting, he was wounded and subsequently lost an eye.

B.A.O.R. WIVES. — So the B.A.O.R. wives get a housing reception? No wonder. Even if they are residents, it is grossly unfair to turn them out of their homes for no good reason. What with keeping the prisoners of war here and now robbing them of their homes, it makes me think that our Government is deliberately fostering bad feeling between our two countries. —TOLERANCE.

TETTENHALL STREET LIGHTING — Can you please tell me why the most important street light on my estate is not switched off in working order? This particular spot is just before you turn into Lower-street, and the post-man-street lamp should light the dark-out part of the road. —R. M. MUIR, 17 Aldersley-road, Tettenhall.

Joining the Terr in 1938 he was commissioned into the K.S.L.I. and who served in India in 1941, also held the rank of Lieutenant - Colonel, and Mr Robert Leslie Gwynne, who joined the Royal Armoured Corps in 1940 rose to the rank of captain, after serving in Burma until 1945 with the Royal Corps of Signals. Mr Robert Gwynne (senior) and his four sons are all engaged in the family business as solicitors.

OLDEST INHABITANT. — The LIBERAL PARTY — I would myself out the folly of my argument that a rejuvenated Liberal party is to be hereby the Liberal party by nothing more than a breakaway party operating within the frame-work of a capitalist industrial system. Its failure was responsible for the creation of the Labour party. Liberalism was a creed based upon the erroneous idea that the needs of the poor could be satisfied whilst the privileges of the wealthy were preserved. It was a creed based upon the fallacy that an owning class and a working class should continue to exist, and this was assumed a social foundation for the modelling of modern society. Whether capitalism is represented in the House of Commons by Toryism or Liberalism, the fate of the workless class is a foregone conclusion. Toryism and Liberalism are two notations from the same regiment. Capitalism, with its cut-throat methods in production and its scramble for markets and raw materials, is the direct cause of war. "Deserl, Rat," supported Labour in order to preserve the peace of the world. Why one crave for the formation of a pro-capitalist party? World capitalism

Death Of Mr. F. F.
Vickers, Salop
N.U.T. Ex-Head

The death has occurred at St George's of Mr Frank F. Vickers, a former head master of St. George's C. of E. Schools, at the age of 72.

Mr. Vickers had been a master of the schools for 47 years until his retirement in 1938.

In 1921 he was president of Shropshire County Association of the N.U.T. and was hon. treasurer of Wrekin Teachers Association for 21 years.

Among his many other activities were: hon. secretary to St. George's Parochial Church Council, manager of C. of E. Schools, president, St. George's C.C., a member and one time president of St. George's Bowling Club, an official of the old St. George's Athletic Sports Committee, a former playing member of the Lilleshall and old Priorslee

NOTES FROM THE

Tonight's Smile

Blonde: When he asked me how old I was I couldn't remember whether I was 24 or 25.
Brunette: So how old did you say you were?
Blonde: Eighteen.

Welcome Sun!

AT the time of writing the sun is shining. I make that statement guardedly. I have said it before only to be let down before noon. But this time there does seem reasonable hope that at long last a few hours of favour us will this time, at least the horizon is not rusted with Katherine

L...n awynne. Barbara Gwynne, wife for five years a member of the W.A.A.F.

Mr A. N. Gwynne, who served with the K.S.L.I. and who was in India in 1941.

Brevities

Miss E. Laurel Fletcher, of Glenorah, Haygate-road, Wellington, a former pupil of the Shrewsbury

---

The *Wellington Journal* 21 August 1946 ('MC in the Post') and notification of Class A Release.

Army Form X.213.

RELEASE CERTIFICATE

OFFICERS OF THE TERRITORIAL ARMY
(Including T.A.R. OF O.).

(CLASS "A" RELEASE IN U.K.)

MAJOR D.H. GWYNNE. MC. (95010)

KING'S SHROPSHIRE LIGHT INFANTRY

The above named has been granted 100 days' leave commencing, 25 April 46 and is, with effect from 3 August 46 , released from embodied service in the Territorial Army under Regulations for Release from the Army, 1945.

Office Stamp.

NOTICE.—This certificate is not valid unless it bears the official War Office stamp showing date of issue.

This document is Government property. Any person being in possession of it without authority or excuse is liable under Section 156(9) of the Army Act to a fine of £20 (twenty pounds), or imprisonment for six months, or to both fine and imprisonment.

IF FOUND.—Please enclose this certificate in an unstamped envelope and address it to the Under Secretary of State, The War Office, London, S.W.1.

With his three younger sons — Leslie, Norman and Dennis — back from the war to help with the family business, Robert Gwynne continued as Senior Partner and did not retire from the practice until 1958. Dennis finally qualified as a Solicitor in 1950.

Dennis's mother Winnie and his oldest brother Reg both died within a few months of each other in May and July 1948, respectively. From the note of concern evidenced in Dennis's letters, her health was already in decline by 1945.

I am not sure what happened with Hilda, but Dennis married Patricia Tristem in 1953. His best man was Alan Benson.

The 10th Gurkha Rifles remained with the British Army post partition in 1947, and in 1949 were renamed 10th Princess Mary's Own Gurkha Rifles. The Battalion stayed on in Burma after the war and was in attendance at the Burmese independence ceremony in Rangoon in January 1948.

Auntie Pat told me that men from the Regiment came over for the Queen's Coronation in June 1953. She said the Gurkhas had hoped to trek to Shropshire to see Dennis. According to Pat and his sister, Barbara, Dennis suffered for a long time with nightmares and insomnia related to his experiences in Burma.

PROBATION OFFICER WEDS

PROBATION Officer for Welling-
ton and eldest daughter of the
late F/Lieut. H. 'H. V. Tristem and
Mrs. Tristem, of Gillingham (Kent),
Miss Patricia Mary Tristem was
married at All Saints' Church, Wel-
lington, on Saturday, to Mr. Dennis
Herbert Gwynne, a local solicitor.
The bridegroom is the youngest son
of Mr. R. Gwynne and the late Mrs.
W. E. Gwynne, of "Eversleigh," Mill
Bank, Wellington.
Given away by her brother (Mr. P.

Tristem), the bride wore a full crino-
line ivory brocade gown patterned with
lilies-of-the-valley motif in gold thread,
a bodice embroidered with pearls,
white beads and diamante, and also a
coronet of pearls and diamante and a
full tulle veil. She carried a bouquet
of lilies, stephanotis, gladioli and
lilies-of-the-valley.
Attendants were the Misses Edna
Rawlings, Nicolette Tristem (sister of
the bride), Pauline Gwynne and Janet
Edwards (nieces of the bridegroom)

and Veronica Whittles, all in full-
length ballerina frocks of white net,
bodices embroidered with silver bead-
ing, coronets of white net embroidered
with pearls, beads and diamante, with
delicate clusters of lilies-of-the-valley
and white lilac. They carried mixed
bouquets of lilies-of-the-valley, cream
roses and stephanotis. Best man was
Mr. A. de C. Benson, and the service
was conducted by the Rev. J. R.
Bournon. A reception was held at the
Forest Glen.

Dennis and Patricia Gwynne on their wedding day in 1953 at St
Peter's, Wrockwardine

*Dennis and Pat were married for nineteen years and
had no children. Dennis died of kidney failure on 20
November 1972 at the age of just 53. His regimental obituary remarked:*

> *Held in the highest affection and respect through-
> out the County, the whole of Shropshire has
> mourned his death...in which we, who knew
> him and valued his friendship so highly, all join.*

DHG after the war with his MG, which he liked to race from the
Red Lion to the White Lion on the old A5

Dennis Gwynne, MC, TD (1919 – 1972)

In my heart it has not died
The war that sleeps on Severn side
They cease not fighting, east and west
On the marches of my breast

From AE Housman's 'A Shropshire Lad'

Acknowledgements

I WOULD LIKE TO thank the 10th Princess Mary's Own Gurkha Rifles Regimental Trust for their kind permission to quote extracts and reproduce certain maps from the *Bugle & Kukri* (Volume 1) by Colonel B.R. Mullaly and also for providing a copy of Dennis's obituary from the Regimental magazine.

Mention must go in particular to D.F. Harding, late 10GR, for his encyclopedic knowledge of the Regiment's history and for filling in so many gaps in my narrative and to Peter Sharland for his many introductions and to Paul Heneker for his invaluable help in bringing Dennis's photos back to life.

I apologise unreservedly if I have unintentionally made errors of fact or omission in my historical narrative about 10GR or their role in the Burma Campaign. It is difficult treading on such hallowed ground.

Thanks also to Julian Pilcher for sharing his detailed knowledge on the history of the construction of the Tiddim Road and especially the role played by the amazing planters of the Indian Tea Association.

I would also like to thank the 3rd Viscount Slim for his kind permission to quote an extract of Field Marshall the 1st Viscount Slim's excellent memoir *Defeat into Victory*. His description of the logistics of supplying troops fighting in the jungle and the impact of disease on the men of the Fourteenth Army is as vivid today as it would have been when it was first written.

I would also like to thank my friend DW for the secret journey he undertook in order to gather material for this book … cross country and with only the stars to navigate by, it was worthy of a Chindit!

And of course, thank you to my father, Michael Gwynne, who provided Dennis's letters and photographs and hopefully enjoyed the hours of family 'fact-checking' as much as I did!

Lastly, huge thanks to Richard Charkin at Mensch Publishing for all his wise advice and in encouraging me to indulge in a lockdown obsession that grew into a book, and to Miranda Vaughan Jones and Philip Beresford for their professionalism and creativity and for giving it all form and substance.